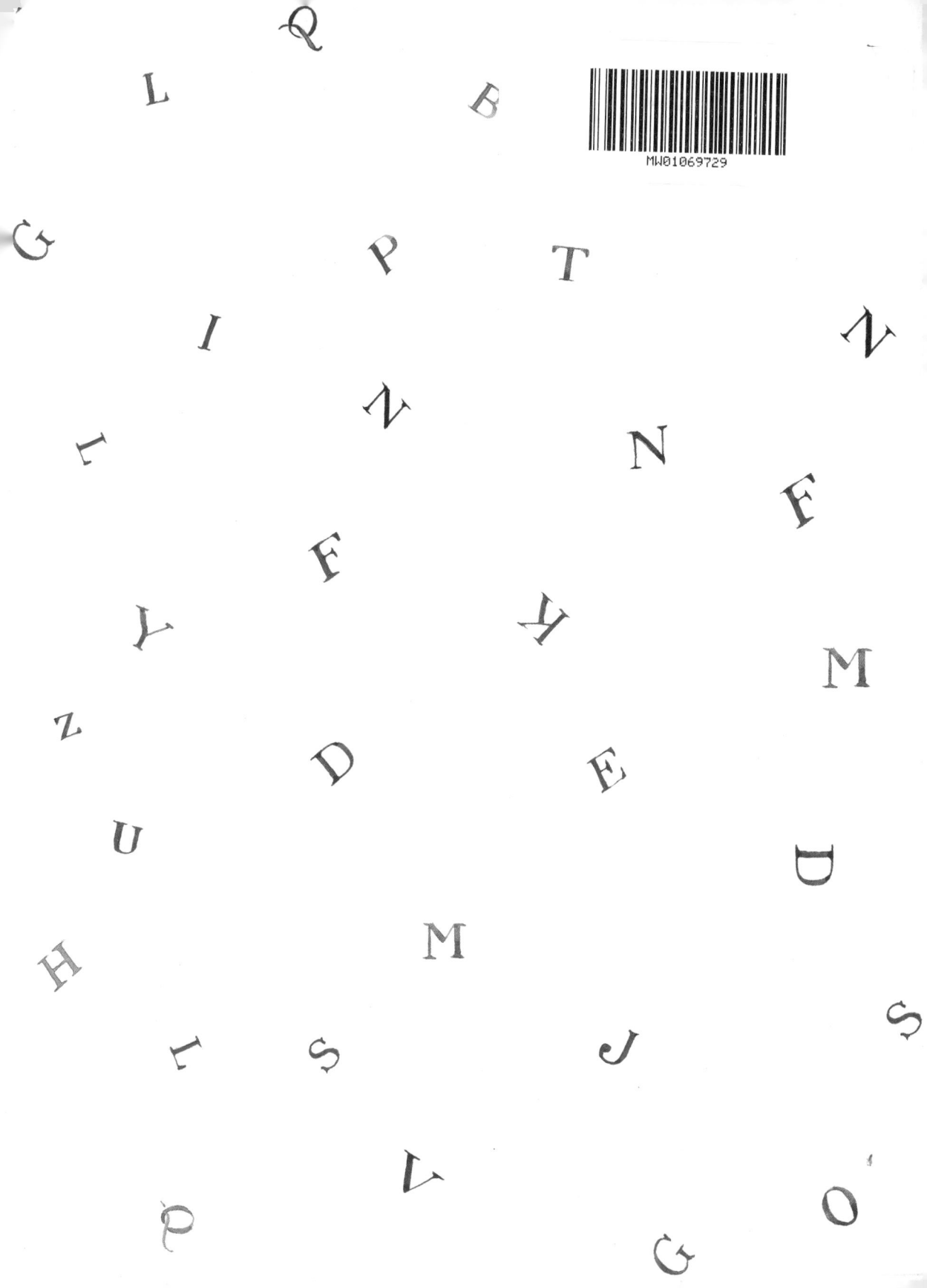

Impossible is just an opinion.
♥ Paul Coelho

"Yearning to be better,
to be more, to give
more, to create more,
to touch more hearts,
to be a Valentine
for the World.
♥ Susan Branch

MY BOOK _____

The sky is filled with stars
Invisible by day. ♥

Henry Wadsworth Longfellow

God sent His singers
upon the earth, with songs
of sadness & of mirth, that they
might touch the hearts of men, &
bring them back to heaven again.
♥ Henry Wadsworth Longfellow

Distilled Genius

Eleanor Roosevelt

The future belongs to those who believe in the beauty of their dreams.
— Eleanor Roosevelt

A Collection of Life-Changing Quotations

SUSAN BRANCH

SPRING STREET Publishing

MARTHA'S VINEYARD · MASSACHUSETTS

FIRST EDITION

ISBN 978-0-9960440-6-6
Library of Congress Control Number
           2022935458

      10 9 8 7 6 5 4 3 2 1

PRINTED IN THE
UNITED STATES OF AMERICA

CONTENTS

A book which has been culled from the flowers of all books. ♡ George Eliot

Someday we'll find it,
the rainbow connection,
the lovers, the dreamers,
and me. ♥ PAUL WILLIAMS

And so it began. . .

PREFACE

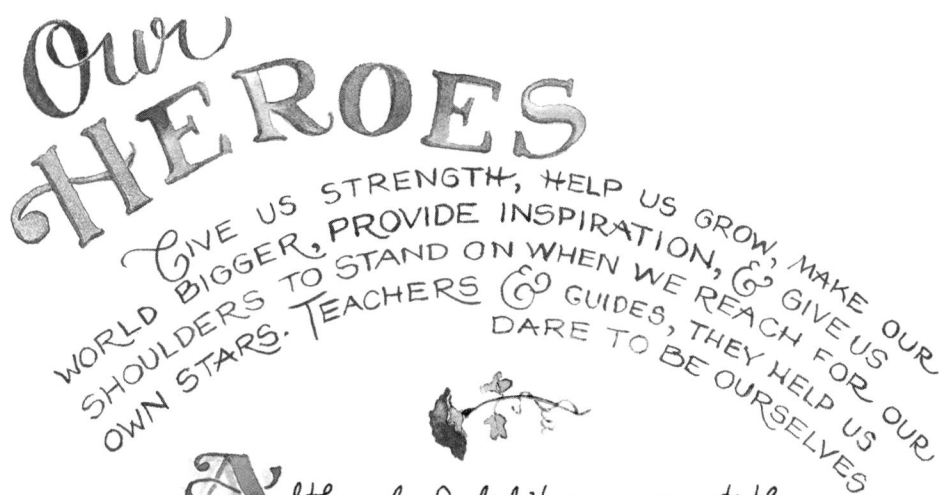

Our HEROES

GIVE US STRENGTH, HELP US GROW, MAKE OUR WORLD BIGGER, PROVIDE INSPIRATION, & GIVE US SHOULDERS TO STAND ON WHEN WE REACH FOR OUR OWN STARS. TEACHERS & GUIDES, THEY HELP US DARE TO BE OURSELVES.

Although I didn't recognize it then, this book has its roots back in 1982, when I was 34, and my husband informed me he was no longer interested in being married. Many of you know this story from my book *Martha's Vineyard, Isle of Dreams*, but for those who don't, & to make a very long story short, it was a terrible time for me, I didn't know what to do with myself. After about six months of public suffering, I wiped my tears, packed up the pieces of my broken heart, & ran away from my home in California, as far as I could go, to Martha's Vineyard, an island off the coast of Massachusetts, 3,000 miles from all I held dear.

I had only planned a 3-month break, removing myself from constant reminders of all I had lost, to try & steady myself. But a week after arriving on the island, I accidentally bought a tiny one-bedroom house in the woods. I still don't know how it happened. It wasn't planned, but I couldn't help it, you would have done it too. Anyway, that's when I found out I was moving away from home forever.

IT WAS LOVE AT FIRST SIGHT.

My heart told me I'd done the right thing, but despite the beauty, history, & charm of my new home, it slowly dawned on me that starting over wasn't something that would happen with a snap of the fingers. I would need the investigative spirit of Dick Tracy to figure it out. ♥

Stranger in a Strange Land

There was healing magic in that little house—in the woods & wild blueberry bushes surrounding it, in the stars & the moon hanging over it, but especially in some of the books left behind by the previous owner. Most fortuitous of all was a thick volume called Bartlett's Familiar Quotations. I'd never seen a book of quotations before, but since I had lots of time on my hands, I started looking through it.

There were practical words of wisdom from the ages, talking to me, from all parts of the world on every subject, from the beginning of time; all of them saying, in their own ways, that I had the power to shape my world! It was thrilling! From the Bhagavad Gita to Anne Frank, Rosa Parks to George Patton, Marcus Aurelius to Helen Keller & everyone in between—thinkers & teachers of all stripes, colors, & creeds, nurturing & life affirming, clever, poetic, heroic, hilarious, & human, because everything that needed to be said HAS been said by someone whose extraordinary life & times give their words fathomless depth. ♥ They gave me Hope. ♥

BUT YOUR SOLITUDE WILL BE A SUPPORT & A HOME FOR YOU, EVEN IN THE MIDST OF VERY UNFAMILIAR CIRCUMSTANCES, AND FROM IT YOU WILL find ALL YOUR PATHS. ♥ RANIER MARIA RILKE

From then on, every time I went to a bookstore, I looked for more quote books. Pretty soon I had a shelf full of them. I read them cover-to-cover, like novels. I took them everywhere, on cross-country train trips & out to lunch, putting stars next to my favorites. I wrote them in pen & ink & watercolor & put them by subject in scrapbooks. Collecting quotes became a lifelong passion, a pure education; I began thinking of these books of soul-satisfying quotations from the smartest people who ever lived as "distilled genius." Textbooks for how to live; they should be in every school library. ♥

Anne Frank

The intellect of the wise is like glass; it admits the light of heaven and reflects it. ♥ Augustus Hare

Mary McLeod Bethune

Reading about the struggles of these people who, against all odds, had made something mean-ingful of their lives made me brave, helped me heal, showed me where to look for my dreams, & encour-aged me to try to make them a reality. They were saying, "If I can do it, you can too." I felt like I was learning the secrets of life. ♥

Believe in yourself, learn, & never stop wanting to build a better world. ♥ Mary McLeod Bethune

Benjamin Franklin

Sometimes a quotation would be so witty, so charming, so smart, I'd get curious about the author & look for biographies & books by or about him or her ~ it was a bonus if they kept a journal. ♥

The appetite grows for what it feeds on. ♥ Ida B. Wells

As time went by, inspiration led to adventure, & now I've visited the homes & gardens of many of my favorites, to walk where they walked, to breathe in the history of people such as Beatrix Potter, Mark Twain, Jane Austen, Abigail Adams, William Morris, Helen Keller, Louisa May Alcott,

— BEATRIX POTTER, & ME, AT HILLTOP ♥ —

Winston Churchill, Abraham Lincoln, William Shakespeare, Rudyard Kipling, & many more. The people who made me want to be a better person. There was no end to the gift I found in that little house so far away, where I'd been so obviously coming all my life. ♥

— Mark Twain —

WE HAVE NOT EVEN TO RISK THE ADVENTURE ALONE FOR ALL THE HEROES of ALL TIME HAVE GONE BEFORE US. ♥ Joseph Campbell

It's been a joy bringing this book to fruition. Never have I felt so much love when working on a book ~ waking up to spirit-strengthening joy words is good for what ails you ~ it put little wings on my feet every day. We've lost so much to history, but these wise words are FOREVER.

— Louisa May Alcott —

It's not that I belong to the past, but that the past belongs to me. ♥ Mary Antin

Indulge your imagination in every possible flight.
J a n e   A u s t e n

Abigail Adams

I know many of you collect quotes too, so I left blank pages at the end of each chapter for you to add your favorites. And there will be a volume two because a 45-year collection doesn't fit in one book! Wonderful quotations about Home, Family, Traditions, Tea, Gardens, Travel, the Seasons, & more, still to come. The geniuses of the world had a lot to say. ♥

Adam was the only man who, when he said a good thing, knew that nobody had said it before him. ♥ Mark Twain

Albert Einstein

Writers & philosophers of the past were lucky ~ they got all the best words first! Dorothy Parker, irritated by a ringing telephone complained, "What fresh hell is this?" You just can't top that! Nothing much left for the rest of us. But that didn't stop me from trying, which is what they would expect from me, my coaches, mentors, & guides. I added my own two-cents, for better or for worse, so you can see what hanging out with genius for a very long time can do for your basic total idiot. I hope you love it! With all my love, Susan Branch

Ida B. Wells

I have no special talent. I am only passionately curious.
The adorable Albert Einstein

INSPIRATION

With stammering lips and insufficient sounds,
I strive & struggle to deliver right
the music of my nature.
♥ Elizabeth Barrett Browning

To live is to be slowly born.
Antoine de Saint-Exupéry

The SECRETS OF LIFE

Put your ear down close to your soul & listen hard. ♥
♥ Anne Sexton

Seek not outside yourself
Heaven is within.
♥ Mary Lou Cook

Joy is not in things, it is in us.
Benjamin Franklin

BE YOUR
OWN BEST
FRIEND

I myself am heaven and hell. ♥ Omar Khayyam 1048-1131

The moment you notice that you are an instrument of God, the moment you become like a hollow flute, the wind will blow through you, and there will be music.
♥ Shri Dhyanyogi

The awakening of consciousness is not unlike the crossing of a frontier—one step and you are in another country.
♥ Adrienne Rich

It's not in the stars to hold our destiny but in ourselves.
♥ Wm. Shakespeare

The wisdom you seek lies within.
♥ Bhagavad Gita (8th century BC)

You who want
knowledge,
seek the Oneness
within.
There you
will find
the clear mirror
already waiting.
♥ Hadewijch II
13th century

HEROES
MEDITATION
NATURE

KEYS to my CASTLE

Not on the outer world
For inward joy depend;
Enjoy the luxury of thought,
Make thine own self friend.
♥ Lydia Howard Sigourney

There is nothing
either good or bad,
but thinking makes it so.
♥ WM. SHAKESPEARE

What you seek is seeking you. ❀ RUMI

Perhaps the beginning is just to say
nice things are going to happen
until you make them happen.
Frances Hodgson Burnett The Secret Garden

NEGLECT NOT THE GIFT
THAT IS IN THEE ♥
I TIMOTHY 4:14

A very little key will open
a very heavy door.
♥ Charles Dickens

The centre that I cannot find
is known to my unconscious mind.
I have no reason to despair
because I am already there.
♥ W. H. Auden

When we argue for our limitations, we get to keep them. ♥ Evelyn Waugh

Run, dear, from anything that may not strengthen your precious budding wings. ♥ Hafez

There are things known and there are things unknown and in between are the doors. ♥ Aldous Huxley

Build, therefore, your own world. ♥ Ralph Waldo Emerson

S mooth seas do not make skillful sailors. ♥ African proverb

The intellect of the wise is like glass; it admits the light of heaven & reflects it. ♥ Augustus Hare

Although I'm only fourteen, I know quite well what I want. I know who is right and who is wrong. I have my opinions, my own ideas and principles, and although it may sound pretty mad from an adolescent, I feel more of a person than a child. ♥ Anne Frank

You hail from dreamland dragon-fly? A stranger hither? So am I. ♥ A. Mary F. Robinson

IF YOU LIKE THE WAY THINGS ARE GOING, JUST KEEP DOING WHAT YOU'RE DOING. ♥ Susan Branch

When you're stuck in a spiral, to change all aspects of the spin, you only need to change one thing. ♥ Christina Baldwin

Everyone's life is a fairy tale written by God's fingers. ♥ Hans Christian Andersen

You are the art & THE ARTIST ♥ Susan Branch

It is a characteristic of wisdom not to do desperate things. ♥ Henry David Thoreau

YOU HAVE TO BELIEVE WE ARE MAGIC, NOTHING CAN STAND IN OUR WAY... ♥ Olivia Newton-John

IF I AM NOT FOR MYSELF, WHO WILL BE FOR ME? ♥ Hillel the Elder 110BC

No one can make you feel inferior without your consent. ♥ Eleanor Roosevelt

You've got to find yourself first. Everything else will follow. ♥ Charles de Lint

SPIRITUAL LOVE IS A POSITION OF STANDING WITH ONE HAND EXTENDED INTO THE UNIVERSE & ONE HAND EXTENDED INTO THE WORLD, LETTING OURSELVES BE A CONDUIT FOR PASSING ENERGY. ♥ CHRISTINA BALDWIN

We did then what we knew how to do. Now that we know better, we do better. ♥ Maya Angelou

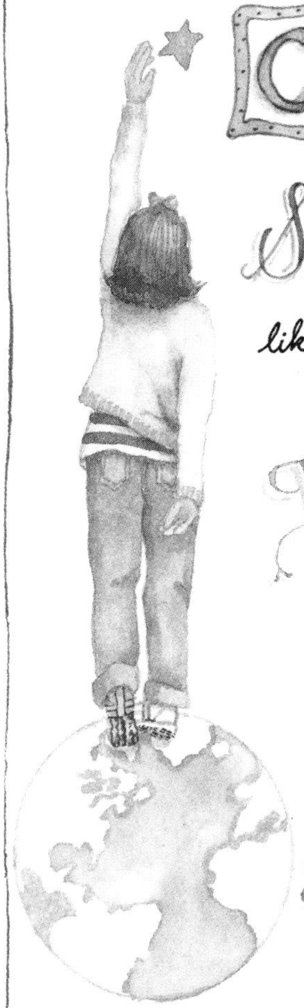

Chance is perhaps the pseudonym of God when He did not want to sign. ♥ Anatole France

Suddenly she spread her brown wings for flight, & soared into the air. She passed the grove like a shadow; & like a shadow, she sailed across the garden. ♥ Oscar Wilde

Very little is needed to make a happy life; it is all within yourself, in your way of thinking. ♥ Marcus Aurelius

WHEN YOU DOUBT YOUR POWER, YOU GIVE POWER TO YOUR DOUBT. ♥ Honoré de Balzac

I think I can... ♥ THE LITTLE ENGINE THAT COULD

Behold! The kingdom of God is within you. ♥ Luke 17:21

Quiet the mind & the soul will speak. ♥ Ma Jaya Sati Bhagavati

I meditate so that my mind cannot complicate my life. ♥ Sri Chinmoy

You have a treasure within you that is infinitely greater than anything the world can offer. ♥ Eckhart Tolle

When you realize there is nothing lacking, the whole world belongs to you. ♥ Lao Tzu

My experience in learning to meditate was like the movie *The Secret Garden*. Up until they opened the door to the walled garden, the film was in black-and-white, but on the other side of the door, it turned to glorious Technicolor. ♥ *Susan Branch*

**T**he real magic is believing in yourself. If you can do that, you can make anything happen. ♥ *J. W. von Goethe*

I am the greatest. I said that before I even knew I was. ♥ *Muhammad Ali*

**B**e true to yourself. ♥ *S.B.*

You are your best thing. ♥ *Toni Morrison*

All the world is made of faith & pixie dust. ♥ *J.M. Barrie*

What is life? It is the flash of a firefly in the night. It is the breath of a buffalo in the wintertime. It is the little shadow which runs across the grass and loses itself in the sunset. ♥ *Crowfoot*

Meditate: Say sweet things to yourself & Count your blessings every day. ♥ *Susan Branch*

I do not ask for any crown but that
which all may win;
Nor try to conquer any world,
except the one within.
Be Thou my guide until I find, led by
a tender hand,
The happy kingdom in myself & dare
to take command.
♥ Louisa May Alcott

It is not easy to find happiness in ourselves, and it is
not possible to find it elsewhere. ♥ Agnes Repplier

Dwell on the beauty of life. Watch the stars
and see yourself running with them.
♥ Marcus Aurelius (Emperor of Rome 161-180 AD)

Wonder is the
beginning of wisdom.
Socrates

Inspiration is everywhere but
becoming AWARE takes
practice. ♥ SB

Heed the small still voice that so seldom
leads us wrong & never into folly.
♥ Mme du Deffand

But if you try sometimes you get what you need.
♥ Rolling Stones

You're only given one little spark of madness. You mustn't lose it.
♥ Robin Williams

We come spinning out of nothingness, scattering stars like dust. ♥ Rumi

Feed your soul

FEED YOUR SOUL

READ THE SEVEN SPIRITUAL LAWS OF SUCCESS by DEEPAK CHOPRA. GET THINKING LIKE LEONARDO DA VINCI and LEARN FASCINATING *Mind Mapping*. ♥ SB

LIFE ISN'T ABOUT FINDING YOURSELF. IT'S ABOUT CREATING YOURSELF.
♥ George Bernard Shaw

SOMETIMES THE WAY TO BE IN TOUCH WITH THE WORLD IS TO BE OUT OF TOUCH. ♥ anon.

Providence wakes each morning an hour before the sun.
French Folktales ♥

"You just think lovely wonderful thoughts," PETER EXPLAINED, *"and they lift you up in the air."* ♥ J. M. Barrie

Hear blessings dropping their blossoms around you.
Rumi

The secret of having it all is believing that you do.
♥ *Susan Branch*

I will prepare & someday my chance will come.
♥ Abraham Lincoln

But all the magic I've ever known,
I had to make myself. Shel Silverstein

Being enough was going to
have to be an inside job.
♥ Anne Lamott

Look within. Within is the
fountain of good,
& it will ever
bubble up
if thou wilt ever dig.
♥ Marcus Aurelius

Be kind, for everyone you meet
is fighting a hard battle.
Socrates

Whatever is true, whatever is honorable, whatever is right,
whatever is pure, whatever is lovely, whatever is admirable—
if anything is excellent or praiseworthy—
think on these things. ♥ Philippians 4:8

Everything has beauty,
but not everyone sees it.
♥ Confucius

You can often change your
circumstances by changing your
attitude. ♥ Eleanor Roosevelt

I could see—they were all saying it—
the secret was within. ♥ JB

A finished person is a boring person.
♥ Anna Quindlen

Still, for all her soaring & sailing through the sky, she had no idea where she was going. ♥ French Folktales

I am an expression of the divine, just as the peach is, just like a fish is. ♥ Alice Walker

You don't have a soul. You are a soul. You have a body. ♥ C. S. Lewis

Love the moment, & the energy of that moment will spread beyond all boundaries. ♥ Corita Kent

Some people like to make a little garden out of life & walk down a path. ♥ Jean Anouilh

I have no special talents. I'm only passionately curious. Albert Einstein

The mind that opens to a new idea never returns to its original size. ♥ Albert Einstein

Don't part with your illusions. When they are gone, you may still exist, but you have ceased to live. ♥ Mark Twain

Curiosity the gift that keeps on giving ♥ SBR

While there's life, there is hope. Be brave, be curious be determined. ♥ Stephen Hawking

All the way to heaven is heaven. ♥ St. Catherine of Siena

ALL HUMAN BEINGS HAVE A GODLIKE, DIVINE POWER, ONLY MOST OF US DON'T TAP INTO IT. ♥ Ruby Dee

Such a sky & such a sun
I never knew & neither did you
and everybody never breathed
quite so many kinds of yes
♥ E. E. Cummings

Every cell in my body is bathed in the light, love, and creativity of God. ♥ Susan Branch

Since we are destined to live out our lives in the prison of our minds, our one duty is to furnish it well. ♥ Peter Ustinov

It's not easy discovering the things that matter . . . but trust that time will bring them. ♥ Susan Branch

Be a lamp, or a lifeboat, or a ladder. ♥ Rumi

Some things have to be believed to be seen. ♥ Madeleine L'Engle

Give yourself a gift: the present moment. ♥ Marcus Aurelius

Don't be ashamed to need help. Like a soldier storming a wall, you have a mission to accomplish. And if you've been wounded and you need a comrade to pull you up? So what? ♥ Marcus Aurelius

Be who you are & say what you feel, because those who mind don't matter, & those who matter don't mind. ♥ Dr. Seuss

Look inside yourself for the answers — you're the only one who knows what's best for you. Everybody else is only guessing. ♥ Charles de Lint

We are only trustees for those who come after us. ♥ William Morris

Not to know what happened before one was born is always to be a child. ♥ Cicero

What we do in life ripples in eternity. ♥ Marcus Aurelius

Learn how to see. Realize that everything connects to everything else. ♥ Leonardo da Vinci

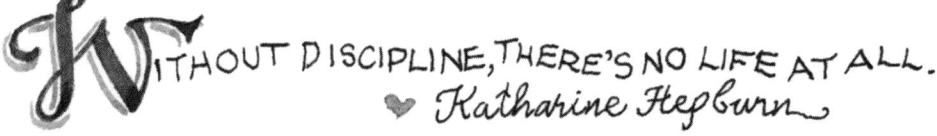WITHOUT DISCIPLINE, THERE'S NO LIFE AT ALL. ♥ Katharine Hepburn

NEVER LIVE FASTER THAN YOUR GUARDIAN ANGELS CAN FLY

KIND WORDS

GOOD BOOKS

The modern rule is that every woman must be her own chaperone. ♥ Amy Vanderbilt

It's a toxic world but YOU HAVE THE POWER to protect yourself. ♥ Feed your life from the well of SWEETNESS. ♥

MUSIC THAT MAKES YOUR SPIRIT SOAR

MOVIES THAT INSPIRE

Everybody gets so much information all day long that they lose their common sense. ♥ Gertrude Stein

♥ Susan Branch

There are only two ways to live your life. One is as though nothing is a miracle. The other is as if everything is.
♥ ALBERT EINSTEIN

What lies behind you & what lies in front of you pales in comparison to what lies inside of you. ♥ Ralph Waldo Emerson

Take time to just think;
let it be cloaked in a daydream.
Let it feel a little bit lonely.
♥ Susan Branch

Our life is what our thoughts make it. ♥ Marcus Aurelius

Hear your inner voice. If it's not saying nice things Change it... It is yours & it is trainable. ♥SB

We need time to dream, time to remember, time to reach for the infinite. Time to be.
GLADYS TABER ♥

It is done onto you as you believe. ♥ MATTHEW 9:29

Go. Be. Love. The world needs you. ♥ SB

From the

THE BIG BOOK OF WELL-KNOWN FACTS

ACCORDING TO THE PLANETS, YOU HAVE GROWN A BIT TOO COMFORTABLE WITH THINGS THE WAY THEY ARE. YOUR LIFE NEEDS SHAKING UP.
Aries horoscope 1987

In order to love who you are, you cannot hate the experiences that shaped you. ♥ Andrea Dykstra

TEACHING & INSPIRING

We live in deeds, not years; in thoughts, not breaths; in feelings, not in figures on a dial. We should count time by heart-throbs. He most lives who thinks most - feels the noblest - acts the best. ♥ P.J. Bailey

With the arrogance of youth, I determined to do no less than to transform the world with Beauty. ♥ William Morris

We're part of the stars & the wind & every flower that blows. ♥ Susan Branch

Never forget: You are the light of the WORLD.

Every wonderful thing is inside you. ♥

♥ Susan Branch

Let us remember: One book, one pen, one child, and one teacher can change the world. ♥ Malala Yousafzai

"Miss Potter" is a wonderful movie, but for the whole magnificent story, read "Beatrix Potter, A Life in Nature" by Linda Lear.

You have within you the strength, the patience, & the passion to reach for the stars, to change the world. ♥ Harriet Tubman

IF I HAD BEEN CAUGHT YOUNG ENOUGH, I COULD HAVE BECOME ANYTHING. ♥ Helen Beatrix Potter

Visit homes & workspaces of
HEROES for INSPIRATION & EDUCATION

The desire to know, to learn, and to grow is the powerhouse of knowledge, wisdom, and discovery. ♥Michael J. Gelb

Shh

Feed your soul
with Silence
that's where Dreams
are born. ♥ SB

In stillness, the world is restored. ♥ Lao Tzu
(4th Century BC)

Slow down, don't move too fast
try to make the moment last. ♥

QUIET

Except for the point, the still point,
There would be no dance,
And there is only the dance.
♥ T. S. Eliot

I seek quiet joys. ♥ John Clare

People need silence like
flowers need sun &
rain. ♥ SB

Go placidly amid the
noise & haste &
remember what
Peace there
may be in
Silence.
The Desiderata

Silence is the music of the soul. ♥ SB

One day you'll wake up and notice the sounds of your house,
the hum of the refrigerator, the sound of the
furnace, and you'll be aware of how deeply your
days have been filled with noise, and how lovely it
is to hear the twitter of birds, the wind in the trees.
♥ Susan Branch

Take a DEEP BREATH of fresh air before going to bed at night: take note of the stars & make a wish for the world. ♡ SB

There is more information in the quiet than in all the computer, TV, & phones in the world because that's how God made us. ♥ SB

I didn't know it, but I needed to be alone. Because, as it turned out, that's where all the secrets were.
♥ Susan Branch

A lively understandable spirit
Once entertained you.
It will come again.
Be still.
Wait.
♥ Theodore Roethke

EVERYTHING IS CONNECTED TO EVERYTHING ♥ SB

Silence is the language of God; all else is poor translation.
♥ Rumi

The solitude of a quiet life stimulates the creative mind.
♥ Albert Einstein

I love that quiet time when nobody's up & the animals are happy to see me.
Olivia Newton-John

When you listen in the woods,
after snow has blanketed
everything,
you hear nothing,
which is so loud it becomes
something.
That's the sound of silence.
Susan Branch

 live in that solitude which is painful in youth, but
delicious in the years of maturity. ♡Albert Einstein

 isten to the silence, it has
so much to say. ♥ Rumi

Outside noisy, inside empty.
♥ Chinese Proverb

HAPPINESS
is the
HARVEST
of the
QUIET EYE
♥ Austin O'Malley

In the quiet, you learn what makes your
heart pound. ♥ *Susan Branch*

LISTEN TO THE WIND

Let us have the luxury of silence.
♥ *Jane Austen*

Listen
to the
Quiet
Where dreams
are born

SHHHH

Have a day of silence—
lie on your bed and
daydream. Fix it so you
hear only nature noises,
cooking noises, page-
turning noises, crackling
fireplace noises, the
skidding of the silver
car as it passes **GO**
& collects $200.⁰⁰ noises.

34

STILLNESS

Speech is silver, but silence is golden. ❤ Muriel Spark

Solitude gives birth to the original in us. ♡ Thomas Mann

PLAY & HAVE FUN

Forget not that the earth delights to feel your bare feet & the winds long to play with your hair.
♥ Kahlil Gibran

Oh Happy Day!

Life is an admirable arrangement. SO clever of it to have a June in every year and a morning in every day . . . let alone things like birds, and Shakespeare.
♥ Elizabeth von Arnim

HAPPINESS

I sound my barbaric YAWP over the rooftops of the world.
♥ Walt Whitman

God respects me when I work, but
He loves me when I sing.
♥ RABINDRANATH TAGORE

The grand essentials of happiness
are: something to do, something
to give, something to love, &
something to hope for.
♥ Susan Branch

HAPPINESS! HA-CHA-CHA!
♥ Louis Armstrong

Blessed are the
happiness makers!
♥ Henry Ward Beecher

Sometimes I need
only to stand
wherever I am
to be blessed.
♥ Mary Oliver

Run mad as often as you chuse,
but do not faint. ♥ Jane Austen

Completely, and Perfectly,
and Incandescently,
Happy.
Jane Austen

To enjoy yourself is the easy method to give enjoyment to others.
♥ L. E. Landon

Something of the most infinite happiness seized upon her heart.
Erik Kelly

I am for everything starting into full-blown perfection at once. Susan Edmonstone Ferrier

JOY ♪ TO THE WORLD

EVERYTHING WAS ACTUALLY

JUST RIGHT

SB

IT IS THE SWEET, SIMPLE THINGS OF LIFE WHICH ARE THE REAL ONES AFTER ALL. ♥ Laura Ingalls Wilder

ONE OF THE SECRETS OF A HAPPY LIFE IS CONTINUOUS SMALL TREATS. ♥ Iris Murdoch

What's the French for FIDDLE-DEE-DEE? ♥ Lewis Carroll

I WAS OVERCOME BY AN ATTACK OF PATHOLOGICAL ENTHUSIASM. ♥ ROBERT LOWELL

HAPPY DAYZZ ARE HERE AGAIN.

To a young heart everything is fun. ♥ Charles Dickens

There is nothing so absolutely bracing for the soul as the frequent turning of one's back on duties. ♥ Elizabeth von Arnim

 Optimism: a cheerful frame of mind that enables a tea kettle to sing though in hot water up to its nose. ♥ Earl Weaver

Nothing great was ever achieved without Enthusiasm. ♥ Ralph Waldo Emerson

On with the dance! Let joy be unconfined. ♥ Lord Byron

Beautiful one day, perfect the next. Motto: Queensland, Australia

The Constitution only guarantees the American people the right to pursue happiness. You have to catch it yourself. ♥ Benjamin Franklin

People are as happy as they make their minds up to be. ♥ Abraham Lincoln

WHAT'S THE DIFFERENCE BETWEEN IGNORANCE & ARROGANCE?
I DON'T KNOW & I DON'T CARE. ♥

FUN is GOOD. ♥

Never play
LeAPFROG
with a
UNICORN

A LITTLE NONSENSE NOW & THEN
IS RELISHED BY THE WISEST MEN. ♥ Roald Dahl

I FIGURE YOU HAVE THE SAME CHANCE OF WINNING THE LOTTERY
WHETHER YOU PLAY OR NOT. ♥ Fran Lebowitz

THERE IS A TIME TO LAUGH & A TIME NOT TO LAUGH
AND THIS IS ONE OF THEM. ♥ Inspector Clouseau

With luck on your side you can do without brains.
Giordano Bruno

BRACE YOURSELF FOR A CLOWN JOKE. OK, READY?
TWO CANNIBALS WERE EATING A CLOWN. ONE
TURNED TO THE OTHER & SAID, "DOES THIS TASTE
FUNNY TO YOU?" (GET IT? FUNNY?)

IF YOU'RE HAPPY & YOU KNOW IT, CLAP YOUR HANDS. ♥

Think of all the beauty still left around you & be happy. ♥ Anne Frank

Happiness grows at our own firesides and is *not* to be picked in strangers' gardens. ♥ Douglas Jerrold

I'm the kind of woman that likes to enjoy herselves in peace. ♥ ALICE WALKER

WHAT TO DO IN CASE OF EMERGENCY:
1. PICK UP YOUR HAT.
2. GRAB YOUR COAT.
3. LEAVE YOUR WORRIES ON THE DOORSTEP.
4. DIRECT YOUR FEET TO THE SUNNY SIDE OF THE STREET.
♥ After Dorothy Fields

Excuse me while I kiss the sky. ♥ Jimi Hendrix

Syllabub, tea, coffee, singing, dancing, a hot supper at eleven o'clock, everything that can be imagined agreeable. ♥ Jane Austen

Let's waltz the rumba. ♥ Fats Waller

The game was to just find
Something about everything
to be Glad about
No matter
What 'twas...
You see, when
You're hunting
for the
Glad things
You sort of
forget the
other kind. ♥

Eleanor Porter, Pollyanna

Barn's burnt down...now I can see the moon.
♥ M a s a h i d e
(A perfect example of the Pollyanna way of thinking.)

Keep good company, read good books,
love good things, and cultivate soul
and body as faithfully as you can.
♥ Louisa May Alcott

It's the choices we make that, in the end,
will define our lives.
♥ Susan Branch

CYNICISM
KILL IT BEFORE IT MULTIPLIES

Laughter through tears is my favorite emotion. ♥ Robert Harling

Give me a moment, because I like to cry for joy. It's so delicious, to cry for joy. ♥ Charles Dickens

Every man's life is a fairy tale written by God's fingers. ♥ Hans Christian Andersen

There is no doubt that running away on a fresh blue morning can be exhilarating ♥ Jean Rhys

The smallest of things can make you feel like something is special about today. ♥ Susan Branch

Spontaneity is a wonderful thing, so it's good to plan for it! Susan Branch

From my Diary

A RED LETTER Day

Read a wonderful book, write a letter, listen to the birds, walk to the pond, nap with the kitties, soak in a bubble bath, wear something cute, paint, knit, sew, cook something wonderful, dig in the garden, watch an old movie, pick a few flowers for a little vase, sing out loud, listen to Tommy Dorsey & Frank Sinatra, make a healthy dinner, sleep with the windows open for sweet dreams. ♥ SB

New Rules

1. Don't take things so seriously.

2. Have more fun.

3. Be brave.

Take deep breaths of marvelous Earth atmosphere.

4. Be spontaneous: go places where something pleasantly unexpected can happen to you.

5. Watch more sunrises & sunsets; wish on moon.

6. Don't complain about the weather.

7. Count your lucky stars.

8. Fill heart with beauty.

9. Go on more picnics.

NETTLE-LEAVED BELLFLOWER

10. Pick more wildflowers (learn their names!)

11. Slow down time by using some to do nothing.

12. As English poet Rupert Brooke suggested:

FLING SELF ON WINDY HILL, LAUGH IN SUN,

KISS LOVELY GRASS

HARK, NOW HEAR THE SAILORS CRY, SMELL THE SEA & FEEL THE SKY; LET YOUR SOUL & SPIRIT FLY, INTO THE MYSTIC. ♥ VAN MORRISON

Even in a time of elephantine vanity & greed, one never has to look far to see the campfires of gentle people.
Garrison Keillor

THE MOON BELONGS TO EVERYONE, THE BEST THINGS IN LIFE ARE FREE

Now & then, in this workaday world, things do happen in the delightful storybook fashion, & what a comfort that is.
Louisa May Alcott

O wonderful, wonderful, most wonderful wonderful! And yet again, wonderful . . .
♥ William Shakespeare

Take life by the lapels and say, "I'm with you kid, let's go!" ♥ Maya Angelou

There are souls in this world who have the gift of finding joy everywhere, and leaving it behind them when they go.
♥ Frederick William Faber

I suppose you can't have everything, though my instinctive response to this sentiment is always, "Why not?" ♥ Margaret Halsey

Happiness makes up in height for what it lacks in length.
♥ Robert Frost

All one really needs is a divinely attractive bed.
♥ Mrs. Winston Guest

IT'S THE LITTLE THINGS
THAT MEAN THE MOST

CONTENTMENT

TRUTH

They dined on mince, & slices of quince, Which they ate with a runcible spoon; And hand in hand, on the edge of the sand, They danced to the light of the moon. ♥ Edward Lear

Teach us delight in simple things.
Rudyard Kipling

One honest John Tompkins, a hedger & ditcher,
Although he was poor, did not want to be richer;
For all such vain wishes in him were prevented
By a fortunate habit of being contented.
♥ Jane Taylor

I feel an earnest & humble desire, & shall do till I die, to increase the stock of harmless cheerfulness. ♥ Charles Dickens

Now and then it's good to pause in our pursuit of happiness and just be happy.
♥ Guillaume Apollinaire

Never underestimate the value

of the little moment.
♥ SB

Make today so awesome, yesterday gets jealous. ♥ Avani Sharma

How to be Happy

FEED the BIRDS

EAT GOOD FOOD

Take Long Walks

BREATHE FRESH AIR

Wear Something Pretty

Read Good Books

GROW FLOWERS

redecorate

Nap with Pets

Soak in Bathtubs

Write in a Diary

SHOW LOVE

Paint Toenails

SEE CHICK FLICKS

Feed your life from the well of SWEETNESS ♥

SB

Joy is a net of love that can catch souls.
♥ Mother Teresa

My heart is like a singing bird.
♥ Christina Rossetti

I seldom think of my limitations & they never make me sad. Perhaps there is just a touch of yearning at times, but it is vague, like a breeze among flowers. ♥ Helen Keller

Take time daily to reflect on all you have. It may not be all you want but remember, someone somewhere is dreaming to have what you have. ♥ Germany Kent

Strange, it is a huge nothing that we fear. ♥ Seamus Heaney

The appetite grows for what it feeds on. ♥ Ida B. Wells

When you arise in the morning, think of what a precious privilege it is to be alive — to breathe, to think, to enjoy, to love. ♥ Marcus Aurelius

THIS IS THE BEST DAY THE WORLD HAS EVER SEEN. TOMORROW WILL BE BETTER.
R.A. Campbell ♥

TAKING GOOD CARE

STRESS · RELIEF

BE YOUR OWN BEST FRIEND

No day is so bad
it can't be fixed
with a nap. Carrie Snow

THE CHALLENGE

IT'S BEEN PROVEN THAT STRESS CAUSES ACTUAL CHANGES TO THE IMMUNE SYSTEM. YIKES!

IT'S CAUSED BY ALMOST EVERYTHING ~ DIVORCE AND DEATH; NORMAL LIFES PRESSURES, FEARS, TOO MUCH T.V. NEWS ~ EVEN HAPPY THINGS LIKE CHRISTMAS, OUTSTANDING PERSONAL ACHIEVEMENT, OR BUILDING A HOUSE.

IF IT GOES ON TOO LONG IT STEALS VITALITY AND CAUSES ILLNESS. IT'S CUMULATIVE AND IT SNEAKS UP ON YOU ~ ESPECIALLY WHEN YOU ARE TOO BUSY TO NOTICE!

SOLUTIONS

EXERCISE AND MEDITATION STRENGTHEN STAMINA. DAILY DOSES KEEP YOU READY IN CASE OF SUDDEN LIFE CHANGES.

BUBBLE BATHS, MASSAGE, BEING WITH FRIENDS, DEEP BREATHING, HEALTHY DIET, HOBBIES & FUN REFRESH THE SPIRIT.

LAUGHTER BUILDS UP THE IMMUNE SYSTEM (GET HOOKED ON FUNNY BOOKS & COMEDIES.)

LEARN TO SAY NO!

TALKING THROUGH PROBLEMS WITH A PROFESSIONAL IS SOOO HELPFUL ~ GETTING PROBLEMS OUT OF THE DARK & INTO THE LIGHT MAKES THEM LESS SCARY. ♥

♥ Susan Branch

LOVE THE ONE YOU'RE WITH

Vitality... the one gift that no art could counterfeit. ♥ Storm Jameson

KEEPING A POSITIVE ATTITUDE ♥.

Health is the thing that makes you feel like now is the best time of the year. ♥ Franklin Pierce Adams

You are the art & THE ARTIST ♥

MIND BODY SPIRIT
VITALITY

TOUCH NATURE EVERY DAY

GARDEN
GROW
Fresh Flowers
Healthy Vegetables

EAT & GROW STRONG
fresh air

EXERCISE FOR ZEST
RELIEVE STRESS
Long Walks

Discipline
gives wings ♥

LOVE
♥

PET THE CATS

SPIRIT
replenish with meditation

FUEL CREATIVITY
TAKE TIME TO DREAM

Do GOOD WORK

CREATE FUTURE
DO IT RIGHT

SOFT TASKS:
Iron & Sew on Buttons.

LIFE'S GIFTS
Arrange Flowers,
Cook, Write in Diary,
Long Bubble Baths, Read,
Sleep in Clean Sheets,
Drink Fresh Water.

LAUGHTER IS FIRST AID FOR STRESS.

TAKE TIME FOR YOURSELF

It's so much fun watching

Fabulous OLD MOVIES

Guaranteed to make you Laugh, CRY, swoon, dream & think.

VIVACIOUS LADY

Shirley Valentine

Muriel's Wedding

Soapdish

Shakespeare in Love

Serendipity

The More the Merrier

Christmas in Connecticut

Suspicion

ROMAN HOLIDAY

Hobson's Choice

The Quiet Man

Indiscreet

PALM BEACH STORY

Top Hat

Also works as antidote to disheartening news reports.

BACHELOR MOTHER

The Bishop's Wife (1947)

Mrs. Miniver

Margie

2005 Pride & Prejudice

How Green was my Valley

Enchanted Cottage

WAKING NED DEVINE

The Major and The Minor

The Young Victoria

THE LADY EVE

Ball of Fire

1935 David Copperfield

Chick Flick Immersion

They say the movies should be more like life ~
I think life should be more like the movies.
♥ MYRNA LOY

Life is hard but so very beautiful. ♡Abraham Lincoln

WE'RE THE NORMAL ONES

TO US

The especial genius of women I believe to be electrical in movement, intuitive in function, spiritual in tendency. ♥ Margaret Fuller

I WOULD LIVE IN A COMMUNIST COUNTRY PROVIDING I WAS THE QUEEN. ♥ STELLA ADLER

Women

Let me not be sad because I am born a woman
In this world; many saints suffer in this way.
♥ Janabai (c.1340)

THERE IS NOTHING
WRONG WITH
THE WORLD THAT
A SENSIBLE
WOMAN COULD
NOT SETTLE
IN AN
AFTERNOON.
♥
JEAN
GIRAUDOUX

Well-behaved women
rarely make history.
♥ LAUREL THATCHER ULRICH

If I have to I can do anything...
♥ HELEN REDDY

There were two ducks; the female
with the brown head & the other
with the green head ~ the unfemale.
♥ DANIELLE RETTINGER – AGE 5

Everything united in her, good understanding,
correct opinions, knowledge of the world,
& a warm heart.   Jane Austen

But the intellect, cold, is ever more masculine than feminine;
warmed by emotion, it rushes toward mother earth, and puts
on the forms of beauty.   ♥ Margaret Fuller

I want to do it because I want to do it. Women
must try to do things as men have tried. When
they fail, their failure must be but a challenge
to others.   Amelia Earhart

All the things I really like to do are immoral, illegal, or fattening.
♥ Alexander Woolcott

The modern rule is that every woman must be her own chaperone.
♥ Amy Vanderbilt

Everyone has inside of him a piece of good news. The good news is that you don't know how great you can be.
♥ Anne Frank

The most terrifying thing any woman can say to me is "Notice anything different?"
♥ Mike Vanatta

It was so cold I almost got married.
♥ Shelly Winters

If you always do what pleases you, at least one person is pleased.
♥ Katharine Hepburn

It takes a long time to be a diva. I mean, you gotta work at it.
♥ Diana Ross

Lead me not into temptation; I can find the way myself.
♥ Rita Mae Brown

"When you see persons slip down on the ice, do not laugh at them.... It is more feminine on witnessing such a sight, to utter an involuntary scream." *Eliza Leslie,* MISS LESLIE'S BEHAVIOR BOOK 1859

Sugar and Spice and Everything Nice

Rabbit said to Owl, "You and I have the brains; the others have the fluff." *Christopher Robin* A.A. MILNE

One never quite allows for the moron in our midst. Agatha Christie

Great minds discuss ideas; average minds discuss events; small minds discuss people. ♥ Eleanor Roosevelt

Do not be so open-minded that your brains fall out. ✳ G.K. Chesterton

Housework, when done correctly, can kill you. ♥

3 CAN KEEP A SECRET IF 2 OF THEM ARE ♥ DEAD. BENJ. FRANKLIN

I'm as pure as the driven slush. Tallulah Bankhead

She's the sort of woman who lives for others~ You can tell the others by their hunted expression~ ♥ C.S. Lewis

"We did then what we knew how to do. Now that we know better, we do better." ♥ Maya Angelou talking to Oprah Winfrey on T.V.

If you would have a woman love you, fill her above the brim with love of her self — all that runs over will be yours.
♥ Charles Colton

Bow down to her on Sunday
Salute her when her birthday comes
♥ Bob Dylan

I'd like to be Queen of people's hearts. ♥♥
Princess Diana

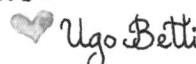

Everyone has, inside himself . . . what shall I call it? A piece of good news! Everyone is . . . a very great, very important character.
♥ Ugo Betti

 have stopped sleeping inside. A house is too small, too confining, I want the whole world, and the stars too.
♥ Sue Hubbell

 "HAVE I GONE MAD?" asked the Mad Hatter. "I'M AFRAID SO," replied Alice. "YOU'RE ENTIRELY BONKERS. BUT I'LL TELL YOU A SECRET. ALL THE BEST PEOPLE ARE.
♥ Lewis Carroll

Her imagination was by habit ridiculously active; when the door was not open it jumped out the window.
♥ Henry James

EDITH WAS A LITTLE COUNTRY BOUNDED ON THE NORTH, SOUTH, EAST & WEST BY EDITH.
♥ MARTHA OSTENSO

To be good, and do good, is the whole duty of mankind comprised in a few words.
♥ Abigal Adams

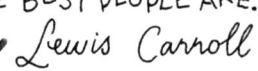 When women are depressed they either eat or go shopping. Men invade another country. It's a whole different way of thinking. ♥ ELAYNE BOOSLER

CAN WE TALK?

Ten measures of speech descended on the world; women took nine & men one. ♥ Babylonian Talmud

I know I chatter on far too much ... but if you only knew how many things I want to say & don't. Give me SOME credit. ♥ L. M. Montgomery

Drawing on my fine command of the English language, I said nothing. ♥ Robt. Benchley

"I may not know much" — another form of locution often favored by her. The tone in which it was spoken utterly belied the words; the tone told you that not only did she know much, but All.
♥ Edna Ferber

It's so easy to be wicked without knowing it, isn't it?
♥ Anne Shirley / L.M. Montgomery

GIRLS WILL BE GIRLS ♥

Woman is the most superstitious animal beneath the moon. When a woman has a premonition that Tuesday will be a disaster, to which a man pays no heed, he will very likely lose his fortune then. This is not meant to be an occult or mystic remark. The female body is a vessel, and the universe drops its secrets into her far more quickly than it communicates them to the male. ♥ Edward Dahlberg

They tell you that you'll lose your mind when you grow older. What they don't tell you is that you won't miss it. ♥ Malcolm Cowley

Why is it that a woman can see from a distance what a man cannot see close? ♥ Thomas Hardy

Very few men care to have the obvious pointed out to them by a woman. ♥ Margaret Baillie Saunders

A woman's guess is much more accurate than a man's certainty. ♥ Rudyard Kipling

'Stay' is a charming word in a friend's vocabulary. ♥ Louisa May Alcott

Next to God, we are indebted to women, first for life itself, & then for making it worth living. ♥ Mary McLeod Bethune

Some beautiful morning she will just wake up, and find it is tomorrow. Not Today but Tomorrow. And then things will happen... Wonderful Things. ♥ L. M. Montgomery

Are you a princess? I said & she said I'm much more than a princess but you don't have a name for it yet here on earth. ♥ Brian Andreas

She was blithe and she was bonnie,
   like the lammie on the lee...
Her heart was warm, her thoughts were pure,
And she was dear to me. ♥ ANON.

Age has given me what I was looking for my entire life ~ it has given me me. I have the life I longed for. I have become the woman I hardly dared imagine I would be.
♥ Anne Lamott

There is entirely too much charm around & something must be done to stop it.
♥ Dorothy Parker

Years are only garments & you either wear them with STYLE all your life, or you go dowdy to the grave.
Dorothy Parker

Charm: the quality in others that makes us more satisfied with ourselves.
♥ Henri-Frédérik Amiel

Who planted daffodils in this rough, briary place? A woman once lived here, a housewife, a poet. We have not forgotten her blueberry pies, her household ways, her verses.
♥ Dionis Coffin Riggs

A study in the Washington Post says that women have better verbal skills than men. I just want to say to the authors of that study, "Duh." ♥ Conan O'Brien

Him: "Wow ~ your purse & your shoes match! How does that happen?" Her: "Witchcraft." ♥ The Marvelous Mrs. Maisel

Pardon my sanity in a world gone insane. ♥ Emily Dickinson

TRUE "POWER" (GIRL, OR OTHERWISE) Comes from Inside

Nothing is impossible to a determined woman. ♥ Louisa May Alcott

YES, I AM WISE, but it's WISDOM BORN of PAIN... ♥ HELEN REDDY

I'm old-fashioned beyond my years. ♥ Muriel Spark

As she realized what she might have been, she grew to be thankful for what she was. ♥ Elizabeth Gaskell

I'm working my way toward divinity. ♥ Bette Midler THE DIVINE MISS M

A woman is the only thing I am afraid of that I know will not hurt me. ♥ Abraham Lincoln

"It's been about 2 months since Shana left & I have yet to make any poor decisions regarding women and/or dating. I'm on a roll. Now if I can just get that mantra down that you assured me would work the next time around: Just do what the woman wants... Just do what the woman wants... Just do what the woman wants..."

♥ EXCERPT FROM MY EX-HUSBAND'S LETTER

There is no charm equal to tenderness of heart. ♥
Jane Austen

Empowered women empower women.
♥ AUTHOR UNKNOWN

If particular care and attention is not paid to the ladies, we are determined to foment a rebellion, and will not hold ourselves bound by any laws in which we have no voice or representation.
♥ Abigail Adams

There came a time when the risk to remain tight in the bud was more painful than the risk it took to blossom. ♥ Anaïs Nin

OUR GREATEST VICTORY IS NOT IN NEVER FALLING, BUT IN RISING EVERY TIME WE FALL. ♥ CONFUCIUS

We can complain because rose bushes have thorns, or rejoice because thorns have roses. ♥ Alphonse Karr

The battle for the individual rights of women is one of long standing and none of us should countenance anything which undermines it.
♥ Eleanor Roosevelt

I know I have the body of a weak and feeble woman, but I have the heart and stomach of a king, and of a king of England too.... ♥ Queen Elizabeth I

in Tickle-Me Pink

It's always something. ♥ Roseanne Roseannadanna

If you have something about yourself that's different, you're lucky. ♥ Taylor Swift

We are not interested in the possibilities of defeat. ♥ Queen Victoria

You wouldn't worry so much about what others think of you if you realized how seldom they do. ♥ Eleanor Roosevelt

It is much easier & often more pleasant, to be a warning rather than an example. ♥ ELIZABETH VON ARNIM

AS GOD IS MY WITNESS, AS GOD IS MY WITNESS, THEY'RE NOT GOING TO LICK ME. I'M GOING TO LIVE THROUGH THIS & WHEN IT'S ALL OVER, I'LL NEVER BE HUNGRY AGAIN. ♥ Scarlett O'Hara

*I*sn't it lovely to be lovely us? ♡ *Nancy Mitford*

FOR MOST of HISTORY, "ANONYMOUS" WAS A WOMAN.
♥ Virginia Woolf

Playmate, come out and play with me,

And we'll be jolly friends forevermore . . . ♥ ♥ attrib. Saxie Dowell

Come.
Sit.
Stay.

TEAPOT'S ON, CUPS ARE WAITING
FAVORITE CHAIRS, ANTICIPATING
NO MATTER WHAT I HAVE TO DO
MY FRIEND, THERE'S ALWAYS TIME FOR YOU. ♥
♥ AUTHOR UNKNOWN

And bring your dollies three, climb up my apple tree,

Shout down my rain barrel, slide out my cellar door,

FRIENDSHIP

Intimacies between women often go backwards, beginning in revelation & ending up in small talk without loss of esteem.
♥ Elizabeth Bowen

Friendship is born at the moment one person says to another, "What? You too? I thought I was the only one."
♥ C.S. Lewis

If you live to be 100, I hope I live to be 100 minus 1 day so I never have to live without you.
♥ Winnie the Pooh

ON THE ROAD BETWEEN THE HOMES OF FRIENDS, GRASS DOES NOT GROW.
♥ NORWEGIAN PROVERB

Friends~they are kind to each other's hopes & cherish each other's dreams.
Henry David Thoreau

A candle passes its fire from wick to wick & loses nothing in the act.
♥ Margot Datz

Constant use had not run ragged the fabric of their friendship.
♥ DOROTHY PARKER

Here at the frontier
the wind is blowing,
although my neighbors
are all barbarians,
And You,
You are a
thousand
miles away...
There are always
two cups at my table. ♥ *Author Unknown*

She openeth her mouth with wisdom; & in her tongue
is the law of kindness. ♥ *Proverbs*

To keep your secret is wisdom,
but to expect others to keep
it is folly. ♥ *Samuel Johnson*

YES'M, OLD FRIENDS IS ALWAYS BEST, 'LESS YOU CAN CATCH A NEW
ONE THAT'S FIT TO MAKE AN OLD ONE OUT OF. ♥ SARAH ORNE JEWETT

If someone betrays you once,
it's their fault, if they
betray you twice, it's your fault.
♥ *Eleanor Roosevelt*

This has been a most wonderful evening. Gertrude has said things tonight it will take her ten years to understand. ♥ Alice B. Toklas

THANK YOU, THANK YOU, NO NO YOU ARE TOO KIND...

The bells of friendship rang.

FRIENDS~

They are kind to each other's HOPES. They cherish each other's DREAMS.
Thoreau

SING: SHE'S VENUS IN BLUE JEANS, MONA LISA IN A PONYTAIL ...
♥ Howard Greenfield

There are people who take the heart out of you & there are people who put it back.
♥ ELIZABETH DAVID

"I often think," she said, "that there is nothing so bad as parting with one's friends. One seems so forlorn without them." ♥ Jane Austen

The simplest pleasures warm true friends most easily. ♥ Alyson Roay

YOUTH IS JUST A MOMENT ~ BUT IT IS A MOMENT YOU CARRY FOREVER IN YOUR HEART. ♥ ANON.

I GET BY WITH A LITTLE HELP FROM MY FRIENDS. ♥ John & Paul

ONE OUT OF EVERY FOUR PEOPLE IN THIS COUNTRY IS MENTALLY IMBALANCED. THINK OF YOUR THREE CLOSEST FRIENDS ~ AND IF THEY SEEM OKAY, THEN YOU'RE THE ONE. ♥ Ann Landers

Birds of a Feather

Oh, the comfort — the inexpressible comfort of feeling safe with a person ~ having neither to weigh thoughts nor measure words, but pouring them all right out, just as they are, chaff & grain together; certain that a faithful hand will take & sift them, keep what is worth keeping, & then with the breath of kindness, blow the rest away.

♥ Dinah Maria Mulock Craik (1866)

♪ Still crazy ♪ After all these years ♪

FOREVER ♥ FRIENDS

A best friend can last your whole life; so when you're old you'll have someone who shares your memories & knew you "when" — then the laughter never has to end. They're easiest to come by when you're young, so if you're 10 & reading this (Hi! ♥), get all the best friends you can & never lose them. Here are some ideas on where to find new friends: Get involved with something that meets regularly & for a long time, so friendship has a chance to develop. Join a book club, or an investment club, sewing or craft classes, creative writing classes, a meditation group, yoga class, or exercise group. You can volunteer to support a candidate, be a Big Sister, put together a fund raiser, be a Girl Scout leader, or join the Junior League. To keep a best friend you have to be nice, be loyal, & be forgiving. To have a best friend you must BE a best friend. To be loved, you must be loveable ♥. The rewards? Support, solace, fun, encouragement, comfort, trust, adventure, love, & laughter.

Be the rainbow in someone's cloud. ♥ MAYA ANGELOU

PLEDGE for a BEST FRIEND

When you are sad,
I will dry your tears.
When you are scared,
I will comfort your fears.
When you are worried, I will give you hope.
When you are confused, I will help you cope.
And when you are lost & can't see the light,
I shall be your beacon, shining bright.
This is my oath, I pledge 'til the end.
Why, you may ask. Because you're my friend.

♥ AUTHOR UNKNOWN

Though miles may lie between us,
we're never far apart,
For friendship doesn't count the miles,
it's measured
in the heart.
♥ Author Unknown

Our roots say we're sisters —
our hearts say we're friends.
♥ ANON.

HELP ONE ANOTHER IS PART OF
THE RELIGION OF OUR SISTERHOOD.
Louisa May Alcott

In the sweetness of friendship let there
be laughter, and sharing pleasures.
For in the dew of little things the heart finds its morning and is refreshed.
♥ Khalil Gibran

Best friends are the secret to life.
♥ Fried Green Tomatoes

THINGS ARE
SO MUCH NICER

THEY MAY FORGET WHAT
YOU SAID, BUT THEY
WILL NEVER FORGET HOW
YOU MADE THEM *feel.* ♥
♥ Carl Buechner

WITH TWO

GIRLFRIENDS FOREVER

I'd walk through fire for my best friend. Hell...not fire,
that would be dangerous. But ~ a super humid room...
but not too humid, because, you know, my hair...
♥ Author Unknown

Heart to Heart
Kindred Spirits
are everything.   ♥ SB

A friend may be waiting behind a stranger's face.
♥ Maya Angelou

We have to be best friends forever ~ you know too much.
♥ Susan Branch

We circled the house endlessly — on scooters, bicycles, pogo-sticks, roller skates & go-cycles; with jump ropes, basketballs, buggies & yo-yos — a continuous stream of children. My 2 best friends & I had known each other forever. ♥ We must have worn a permanent groove in the sidewalk as we went round & round our block, first as little girls in tutus on skates, then as pre-teens, confiding, planning & dreaming out loud our romantic dream of life.

By that time our interests were all-consuming, all-momentous — there was no tomorrow — for us there was only NOW. ♥ We had the wonderful freewheeling ability to think almost anything was funny (remember?), to laugh till we cried (or worse! :)) & in the laughter & the tears (wasn't it Fun?) we formed a bond un-breakable. Best Friends!

♥ Susan Branch

It is much easier & often more pleasant, to be a warning rather than an example. ♥ ELIZABETH VON ARNIM

A toast to us my good fat friends,
To bless the things we eat;
For it has been full many a year,
Since we have seen our feet:
Yet who would lose a precious pound,
By trading sweets for sours?
It takes a mighty girth indeed,
To hold such hearts as ours!
♥ Wallace Irwin

Their conversation ran like a river, splashing, dashing, and glittering in the sun. ♥ Nancy Mitford

One sure way to lose another woman's friendship is to try to improve her flower arrangements. ♥ Marcelene Cox

Everyone has, inside himself . . .
what shall I call it? A piece
of good news! Everyone is . . .
a very great, very important
character.
♥ Ugo Betti

IF FRIENDS WERE FLOWERS I'D PICK YOU

77

LAVERNE & SHIRLEY · MARY & RHODA

WE CRY IN OLD
MOVIES
WE SING IN
THE CAR ♪
WE CALL AT JUST
the RIGHT MOMENT
CHOCOLATE R-US!
WE KNOW THE
DIFFERENCE
BETWEEN THE
TIME FOR
TEA & THE TIME
FOR WINE . . . Susan Branch

YOU & ME · BETTY & WILMA · GAIL & OPRAH

ROSIE & MADONNA · BETTY & VERONICA

LUCY & ETHEL · THELMA & LOUISE

It is one of the blessings of old friends that
you can afford to be stupid with them.
♥ Ralph Waldo Emerson

LOVE IS BLIND. FRIENDSHIP IS CLAIRVOYANT. ♥

'Stay' is a Charming word in a friend's Vocabulary ♥

"I don't feel very much like Pooh today," said Pooh.

"I'll bring you tea and honey till you do," said Piglet.
♥ A. A. MILNE

Women's friendships are like a renewable source of power.
♥ Jane Fonda

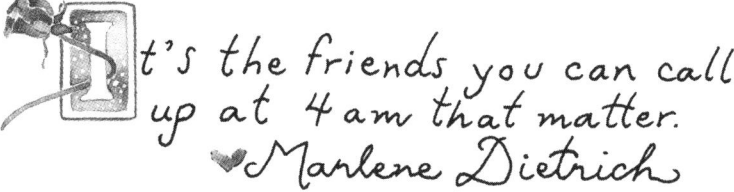

A JOY SHARED IS A JOY DOUBLED

It's the friends you can call up at 4 am that matter.
♥ Marlene Dietrich

To get the full value of a Joy
You must have Somebody
to divide it with.
Mark Twain ♥

AND THE SONG, FROM BEGINNING TO END, I FOUND IN THE HEART OF A FRIEND. ♥ HENRY WADSWORTH LONGFELLOW

WE WENT SHOPPING · WE KEPT SECRETS · WE PLAYED HOPSCOTCH · WE LAY IN THE SUN · WE WENT DANCING · WE HAD TEA · WE WORE MINI SKIRTS · WE SANG IN THE CAR · WE ATE FRENCH FRIES · WE BORROWED CLOTHES · WE CRUISED FOR GUYS · WE WENT TO LUNCH · WE TRIED ON HATS · WE WENT TO PARIS · WE LIP SYNCED · WE LAUGHED SOOOOO HARD ·

My girlfriend Margot came over looking sooo cute. When I told her she said, "I did it for you."
♡ Susan Branch

Women are most fascinating between the ages of 35 and 40 after they have won a few races & know how to pace themselves. Since few women ever pass 40, maximum fascination can continue indefinitely. ♥ Christian Dior

BEAUTY CLOTHES & STYLE

Beauty is as beauty does. ♥ SB

To be forever beautiful: at exactly sunrise on the first of May go outside and roll naked in the dew. ♥ SB

Have you done something jolly with your hair? ♥ Sir Anthony Strallan *Downton Abbey*

I can live for two months on a good compliment. ♥ Mark Twain

Martha Washington wore a yellow dress and lilac slippers on her wedding day.

There is another reason for dressing well, namely that dogs respect it & will not attack you in good clothes. ♥ Ralph Waldo Emerson

Beware of all enterprises that require new clothes. ♥ Henry David Thoreau

Clothes make the man. Naked people have little or no influence in society. ♥ Mark Twain

Though we travel the world over to find the beautiful, we must carry it with us, or we find it not. ♥ Ralph Waldo Emerson

83

Oh, how I regret not having worn a bikini for the entire year I was twenty-six. If anyone young is reading this, go, right this minute, put on a bikini, and don't take it off until you're thirty-four. ♥ Nora Ephron

BEAUTY IS ALSO TO BE FOUND IN A DAYS WORK. ♥ MAMIE SYPERT BURNS

Look closely, the beautiful may be small. ♥ Immanuel Kent

PROVERB
BEAUTIFUL WOMAN WITH A VACANT MIND IS GOOD ONLY FOR FRIGHTENING FISH WHEN SHE FALLS INTO THE WATER. ♥

Beautiful faces are those that wear Whole-souled honesty printed there. ” ♥ Ellen Palmer Allerton

When you got it, flaunt it!

Style is to see beauty in modesty. Andrée Putman

High heels were invented by a woman who'd been kissed on the forehead. ♥ Christopher Morley

Women sit or move to and fro, some old, some young. The young are beautiful — but the old are more beautiful than the young. ♥ Walt Whitman

I was in a beauty contest once. I not only came in last, I was hit in the mouth by Miss Congeniality. ♥ Phyllis Diller

Build a ladder to the stars & climb up every rung & may you stay forever young. ♥ Joan Baez

I BELIEVE IN ACCESSORIES

I bought a dress, a romantic dress, a purely summer party dress: white, splashed with large pink dots, a floppy full skirt and bared shoulders. A dress for a summer tan, a summer dance. ♥ Alice Adams

He's always asking: "Is that new? I haven't seen that before." It's like, why don't you mind your own business? Solve world hunger. Get out of my closet. ♥ Michelle Obama

ENERGY IS MORE ATTRACTIVE THAN BEAUTY... ♥ Louisa May Alcott

There are no bad pictures; that's just how your face looks sometimes. ♥ Abraham Lincoln

Please don't hate me 'cuz I'm beautiful! ♥ ANON.

Natural Beauty

What is self respect? You could write a book! But basically it's the care of character & conduct. Treating yourself like you MATTER, with esteem. Eating healthy food, exercising, getting regular medical check ups, developing spirituality, learning about money, using manners, keeping a clean house ~ self respect makes you beautiful at any age. ♥
♥ Susan Branch

ALWAYS WEAR CLEAN UNDERWEAR IN CASE YOU'RE IN AN ACCIDENT.
♥ My mom

Self respect is a question of recognizing that anything worth having has its price.
♥ Joan Didion

Beauty might bring happiness but happiness always brings beauty. ♥ Nicki Minaj

I base my fashion taste on what doesn't itch.
♥ Gilda Radner

The advantage of doing one's praising for oneself is that one can lay it on so thick and exactly in the right places. ♥ Samuel Butler

Beauty is health. Health is beauty.
♥ Andre Leon Talley

Do I love you because you're beautiful or are you beautiful because I love you? ♥ *Richard Rogers*

There is a garden in her face
Where roses and white lilies grow.
♥ *Thomas Campion*

Taught from infancy that beauty is a woman's scepter, the mind shapes itself to the body, and roaming 'round its gilt cage, only seeks to adorn its prison.
♥ Mary Wollstonecraft 1792

Styles, like everything else, change. Style doesn't.
♥ LINDA ELLERBEE

Beauty is God's handwriting. ♥ *Ralph Waldo Emerson*

The emerging woman will be strong-minded, strong-hearted, strong-souled, and strong-bodied . . . strength and beauty must go together. ♥ Louisa May Alcott

Beauty is being the best you can be.
♥ SUSAN BRANCH

As we grow old, the beauty steals inward.
♥ Ralph Waldo Emerson

Everything you love is beautiful ♥ *Susan Branch*

BUTTONS and BOWS

How we put ourselves together can be very revealing as to what kind of person we are. Here are a few little things you can do with your clothes to make the whole process more interesting & at the same time express your joie de vivre, confidence & energy you 100% original thing you! ♥

TWIST A LONG SCARF THROUGH BELT LOOPS ON BAGGY PANTS (ESPECIALLY LINEN PANTS) A LA FRED ASTAIRE ♥.

DOUBLE OPERA-LENGTH PEARLS OR BEADS AROUND YOUR NECK & HOOK TOGETHER WITH A LARGE BROOCH.

TIE A PRETTY PIECE OF RIBBON (FRENCH OR OTHERWISE) ROUND & ROUND & ROUND YOUR WRIST; TUCK IN ENDS OR LEAVE THEM OUT. WEAR IT PLAIN, WITH A BRACELET, OR PIN A BROOCH ONTO IT. ♥

MY SISTER MARY LOOKS ADORABLE IN SHORT DRESSES OVER PANTS. ♥

ANKLE RIBBON

FANCY PANTS
FOR JEANS, EMBROIDER FLOWERS OR BUTTERFLIES ON POCKETS & HEMS. ADD FABRIC BORDER TO HEMS. FOR CAPRIS: CUT OFF HEMS OF BLACK PANTS, TRIM W/ LACE OR FRINGE ~ JEWEL TRIM ~ RHINESTONE TEARDROPS! GET TRIMS AT FABRIC OR CRAFT STORES.

← SPARKLE ♥!

ALWAYS ALWAYS ALWAYS WEAR TOENAIL POLISH IN THE SUMMER (ONE COAT PRACTICALLY LASTS ALL SUMMER!) TOE RINGS CAN BE CUTE (THUMB RINGS TOO) & PAINTING EACH NAIL A DIFFERENT COLOR IS FUN FOR THE BEACH. ♥

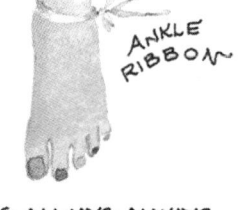

MADE OF CLOTH LOOK EXTRA ADORABLE PINNED WITH FLOWERS OR AN ANTIQUE PIN, ♥ & YOU CAN DO THE SAME THING WITH A SCARF IN YOUR HAIR.

HEADBANDS

88

A WAIST IS A TERRIBLE THING TO MIND, SO IF YOU DON'T REALLY HAVE ONE, LOOK FOR DRESSES WITH LOWER OR HIGHER (EMPIRE) WAISTLINES. ♥ SHOULDER PADS ALSO MAKE YOU LOOK LIKE YOU HAVE A WAIST. ♥ ALL ONE COLOR, SHOES, TIGHTS, SKIRT, JACKET, WILL THIN AND L E N G T H E N YOU~ THEN TIE ON A GREAT SCARF OR NECKLACE TO BRING ATTENTION TO YOUR GORGEOUS FACE, BEAUTIFUL SMILE, AND TWINKLING EYES. ♥

Eye Candy

I LEARNED THIS FROM 1950'S TEEN-AGE MOVIES ~ THAT A BEAUTIFUL FINE GAUGE CARDIGAN SWEATER CAN BE VERY CUTE TURNED AROUND & BUTTONED UP THE BACK. ♥

SEW SPARKLEY BUGLE BEADS ON FOR DRESS-UP ♥

Little Snax:
BIGGER SLAX.

NOTICE TO WOMEN'S CLOTHING STORES OF AMERICA:

IF YOU WOULD PLEASE REMOVE FLUORESCENT LIGHTING FROM THE DRESSING ROOMS, YOU WOULD SELL A LOT MORE BATHING SUITS.
SPEAKING FOR THE WOMEN OF AMERICA ~

I thank you ♥

CLEAN YOUR HAIRBRUSH OUTSIDE SO BIRDS CAN MAKE NESTS FROM YOUR TOUSLES. ♥

FLAT FRONT PANTS CONTROL A POOCHIE STOMACH BETTER THAN PLEATED PANTS (WHICH JUST SEEM TO ALLOW FOR THE PLACE TO PUT THE POOCH! ♥).

Beauty is eternity gazing at itself in the mirror. But you are eternity and you are the mirror.
♥ Kahlil Gibran

When shopping, ask yourself, "is this fad or classic?" Classic is timeless & you'll wear it FOREVER, so that's where the money should go: sunglasses, jeans, jacket, purse, shoes, & HAIRCUT ~ the things you wear everyday are the most important. But fads are fun & FUN is GOOD. ♥

Reality is something you
rise above. ♥ Liza Minnelli

NEWS FLASH
1972: THE FIRST WOMAN
FALLS OFF HER CORK SANDALS.
MILLIONS FOLLOW.
♥ Vogue

If there were dreams
to sell,
Merry and sad to tell,
And the crier rung
his bell,
What would you buy?

♡ Thomas Beddoes

FINDING YOUR DREAMS

IF YOU CAN DREAM IT

YOU CAN MAKE IT SO.

YOU GOT-TO HAVE A DREAM
IF YOU DON'T HAVE A DREAM
How YA GON-NA MAKE A DREAM COME TRUE?
HAPPY TALK

Because nothing happens unless
first we dream. ♥ CARL SANDBURG

And the dreams that you dare to dream really Do Come TRUE...

Someday we'll find it,
the rainbow connection,
the lovers, the dreamers,
and me. ♥ PAUL WILLIAMS

Which would you rather be if you had the
choice—divinely beautiful, dazzingly
clever, or angelically good?
♥ L. M. Montgomery

Listen to the Quiet

Where dreams are born

THERE ARE NO RULES OF ARCHITECTURE FOR A
CASTLE IN THE CLOUDS. ♥ G.K. CHESTERTON

THERE IS NO SUCH THING AS A HOPELESS DREAMER.
IT'S AN OXYMORON. ♥ SB

I want to do something splendid ... something heroic or wonderful that won't be forgotten after I'm dead... I don't know what, but I'm on the watch for it and mean to astonish you all someday. ♡ Louisa May Alcott

IMAGINATION is the main weapon in the WAR against reality. ♡ C.S. Lewis

You are never too old to set another goal or to dream a new dream. ♥ C.S. LEWIS

Laughter is timeless; Imagination has no age; DREAMS are forever. ♥ Walt Disney

Go bravely in the direction of your dreams. ♥ after Henry David Thoreau

So come with me where dreams are born & time is never planned. J.M. Barrie

Hitch your wagon to a star. ♥ Emerson

The future belongs to those who believe in the beauty of their dreams. ♥ Eleanor Roosevelt

Never let anyone tell you magic doesn't exist or that fairies aren't real. It isn't cynicism that will change the world. ♥ SUSAN BRANCH

MAY YOUR EVERY WISH BE GRANTED. ♥ ANCIENT CHINESE curse.

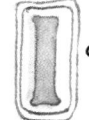I dreamed a dream last night, of stars you could touch, so lovely that when I waked, I cried to dream again.
♥ *William Shakespeare*

Reach high, for stars lie hidden in your soul.

Dream deep, for every dream precedes the goal.
♥ *Pamela Vaull Starr*

Second star to the right...and straight on 'til morning.
James Barrie (Peter Pan)

You can always chase a dream but it will not count if you never catch it. ♥ Malcolm X

BRACE YOURSELF, THE THINKABLE HAS HAPPENED.
♥ *Stephen Colbert*

But once in a while the odd thing happens, once in a while the dream comes true.
♥ W. H. Auden

Don't be afraid of the space between your dreams and reality. If you can dream it, you can make it so.
Belva Davis

All my life I've been circling & circling the tower of the Lord & I still don't know if I'm a poet, a storm, or a song. ♥ Anon.

You have to believe we are magic, nothing can stand in our way... ♥ Olivia Newton-John

You have to dream things out. It keeps a kind of an ideal before you. You see it first in your mind and then you set about to try and make it like the ideal. If you want a garden, why, I guess you've got to dream a garden. ♥ Bess Streeter Aldrich

The imagination needs moodling,~long, inefficient, happy idling, dawdling and puttering. ♥ Brenda Ueland

Dreaming, after all, is a form of planning ♥ Gloria Steinem

E.T. began with me trying to write a story about my parents' divorce. ♥ Steven Spielberg

Pray to God but continue to row toward shore.
♥ Russian Proverb

Things that haven't been done before,
Those are the things to try;
Columbus dreamed of an unknown shore
At the rim of the far-flung sky.
♥ Edgar Guest

In my little house all alone, I could play Shirley Temple
and Fred Astaire music, watch old movies, read, and
pretend that what happens out there in the real world,
doesn't. I wanted a little square box of a life, where I could
put in all the things I loved, get in and close the lid. ♥ SB

"You may say I'm a dreamer,
but I'm not the only one ...
♥ John Lennon

You were born to be an original. Don't die a copy. ♥ John Mason

Be brave, Dream your dreams. Nothing ever stays the same... ♥ SB

Light tomorrow with today.

lways remember that you are absolutely
unique. Just like everyone else.
♥ Margaret Mead

Catch
on fire
with
enthusiasm
& people will
come for miles to
watch you burn.
John Wesley

·LIFE·WORK· ·PASSION·

All we have to decide is what to do with the time that is given us. ♥ J.R.R.Tolkien

Your work is to discover your work & then, with all your heart, give yourself to it. ♥ Buddha

To begin, begin. ♥ Wm. Wordsworth

You can get what you want or you can just get old. ♥ BILLY JOEL

The real magic is believing in yourself. If you can do that, you can make anything happen. ♥ J. W. von Goethe

Whatsoever thy hand findeth to do, do it with thy might... ♡ Ecclesiastes 9:10

You're braver than you believe, stronger than you seem, and smarter than you think. ♥ A.A. Milne

A word grows to a thought ~ a thought to an idea ~ an idea to an act. The change is slow; the Present is a sluggish traveler loafing in the path Tomorrow wants to take. ♥ Beryl Markham ✳ ✳ ✳

So far life had just happened to me. I had to figure out a way to happen to it. ♥ Susan Branch

The Secret of Success is constancy of Purpose. ♥ Disraeli

The meaning of life is to find your gift,
the purpose of life is to give it away.
♥ Pablo Picasso

What we need are more people that specialize in the impossible. ♥ Theodore Roethke

Heart is what determines our fate. ♥ Isabel Allende

♪ Just make your mind up from the start ♪
that the song's gotta come from the heart...
♥ Jimmy Durante

Let the beauty of what you love be what you do. ♥ Rumi

Be not afraid of greatness. ♥ Wm. Shakespeare

What isn't tried won't work. ♥ Claude McDonald

When you doubt your power, you give power to your doubt. ♥ Honoré de Balzac

SHE KNEW EXACTLY WHAT SHE WANTED OUT OF LIFE, WHICH, IN A WORD, WAS EVERYTHING. Dawn Powell

One person with passion is better than forty people merely interested. E.M. Forster

There ain't no rules around here, we're trying to accomplish something. Thomas Edison

Success consists of going from failure to failure without loss of enthusiasm. Winston Churchill

Neglect not the gift that is in thee. I TIMOTHY 4:14

FIRST SAY TO YOURSELF WHAT YOU WOULD BE; THEN DO WHAT YOU HAVE TO DO. Epictetus

LOGIC? GOOD GRACIOUS! WHAT RUBBISH! E.M. Forster

Fame is a bee. It has a song, It has a sting, Ah, too, it has a wing. Emily Dickinson

Logic will get you from A to B. Imagination will take you everywhere. Albert Einstein

Imagination is more important than knowledge. Albert Einstein

The end is nothing, the road is all. Willa Cather

BABY STEPS

I hope we don't lose sight of one thing—that it all started with a mouse. ♥ Walt Disney

Be faithful in small things because it is in them that your strength lies.
♥ Mother Teresa

Thinking small is a tricky way of starting something big.
♥ Susan Branch

All I was trying to do is get home from work.
♥ Rosa Parks

Yard by yard, its very hard, but inch by inch, it's a cinch.
♥ Author unknown

After that, work & hope. But never hope more than you work.
Beryl Markham

Reality is something you rise above. ♥ Liza Minnelli

To love what you do and feel that it matters— how could anything be more fun?
♥ Katharine Graham

Life is like a chess game. Before you take your fingers off your man, be sure you have some idea of what will happen to him three moves from now. ♥ *Susan Branch*

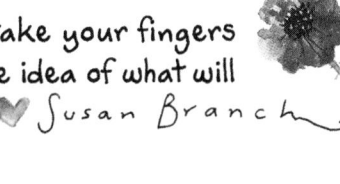

I got my start by giving myself a start. ♥ Madam C.J. Walker 1867-1919

Resolved to take fate by the throat & shake a living out of her. ♥ Louisa May Alcott

BUT A GENTLEWOMAN IS NOT ABLE TO SPIN GOLD OUT OF STRAW; IT REQUIRED A FULL PRINCESS TO DO THAT. *Ivy Compton-Burnett*

I HAVE ALWAYS BEEN BOSSY. ♥ *Shirley Temple*

I believe in hard work. It keeps the wrinkles out of the mind & the spirit. ♥ *Helena Rubinstein*

In a time lacking in truth and certainty, filled with anguish and despair, no one should be shamefaced in attempting to give back to the world, through their work, a portion of its lost heart. ♥ *after Louise Bogan*

Self-development is a higher duty than self-sacrifice.
Elizabeth Cady Stanton

Organization is the key to success
♥ Patricia Stewart (My mom)

Tomorrow was her birthday, & she was thinking how fast the years went by, how old she was getting, & how little she seemed to have accomplished. Almost 25 & nothing to show for it.
♥ Louisa May Alcott

History will be kind to me for I intend to write it myself.
♥ Winston Churchill

I'M NOT AFRAID, I WAS BORN TO DO THIS.
♥ Joan of Arc

Obsession can be wonderful...
♥ SB

Flitting from error to error one discovers the entire truth.
♥ Sigmund Freud

Our PASSIONS, along with CURIOSITY, can turn us into bona fide experts without spending one day in the classroom.
♥ Susan Branch

♫ ...if all of your dreams survive, destiny will arrive...
♥ Olivia Newton John

NEVER GIVE UP NO NO NEVER EVER

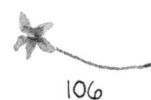

It's believing in roses that makes them bloom.
♥ French proverb

Nothing will come of nothing, we must dare mighty things.
♥ Wm. Shakespeare

We are all failures –
at least the best of us are.
♥ J. M. Barrie

Excellence does not
require perfection.
♥ Henry James

Have no fear of perfection – you'll never reach it.
♥ Salvador Dali

The most successful people
are those who are good
at plan B. ♥ James Yorke

You will do foolish things, but do them with enthusiasm.
♥ Colette

If & when were planted & nothing grew.
♥ Proverb

No pessimist ever discovered the
secrets of the stars, or sailed
to an uncharted land, or opened a
new heaven to the human spirit.
♥ Helen Keller

If A is success in life, then A equals X plus Y plus Z.
Work is X; Y is play; and Z is keeping your mouth shut.
♥ Albert Einstein

Where there's a will there's a way.
♥ My Mom

Do your best but after that embrace the words "GOOD ENOUGH."
♥ Susan Branch

The best time to plant an oak tree is twenty-five years ago. The second best time is now. ♥ Chinese proverb

Take life by the lapel and say, "I'm with you kid, let's go!" Maya Angelou ♥

The best way to find yourself is to lose yourself in the service of others.
♥ Mahatma Gandi

Learn to say 'no' to the good so you can say 'yes' to the best.
♥ John C. Maxwell

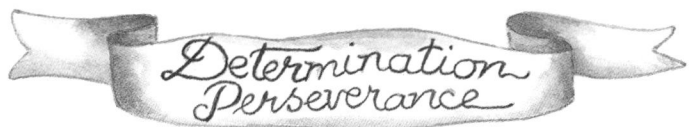
Determination Perseverance

I have not failed. I have successfully discovered twelve hundred ideas that don't work.
♥ Thomas Edison

Above all, be the heroine of your own life.
♥ Nora Ephron

I am so full of my work, I can't stop to eat or sleep, or for anything but a daily run. ♥ Louisa May Alcott

If you like the way things are going, keep doing what you're doing.
♥ ANON.

Remember, the scenery only changes for the lead dog.
♥ after Louis Grizzard

Don't just wait & trust to fate
& say, that's how it's meant to be.
It's up to you how far you go,
If you don't try you'll never know.
And so my lad as I've explained
Nothing ventured, nothing gained.

Merlin, Sword in the Stone. The Sherman Brothers

Go not to the Elves for counsel, for they
will say both no & yes. ♥ J. R. R. Tolkien

Only from the heart
can you touch
the sky. ♥ Rumi

Well done is
better than
well said. ♥
Benjamin Franklin

Everything you can imagine
is real. ♥ Pablo Picasso

A man should choose
with a careful eye
the things to be
remembered by.

Robert P. T. Coffin

Things won are done,
Joy's soul lies in
the doing.
♥ Shakespeare

Luck is not a business model. ♥ Anthony Bourdain

Carpe diem; sieze the day, boys;
make your lives extraordinary."
♥ ROBIN WILLIAMS WHISPERS IN DEAD POET'S SOCIETY.

There's a fine line between GENIUS & INSANITY. I have erased this line. ♥ Oscar Levant

It's so simple to look wise: Just think of something stupid to say, and then, don't say it. ♥ Sam Levenson

HE IS A MOST REMARKABLE MAN; BETWEEN US WE COVER ALL KNOWLEDGE; HE KNOWS ALL THERE IS TO KNOW, & I KNOW THE REST.

Mark Twain

LIGHT TOMORROW WITH TODAY. ♥

Elizabeth Barrett Browning

EXPERIENCE IS A BRUTAL TEACHER, BUT YOU DO LEARN. ♥ C. S. Lewis

Every artist was first an amateur. ♥ Ralph Waldo Emerson

The harder you work, the luckier you get. ♥ Gary Player

BE CAREFUL WHAT YOU SET YOUR HEART ON, FOR IT WILL SURELY BE YOURS. ♥ Ralph Waldo Emerson

All life is an experiment. The more experiments you make the better. ♥ Ralph Waldo Emerson

COMMON SENSE IS INSTINCT, ENOUGH OF IT IS GENIUS. George Bernard Shaw

BE YOURSELF. EVERYBODY ELSE IS ALREADY TAKEN. ♥ Oscar Wilde

A society grows great when old men plant trees whose shade they know they shall never sit in. ♥ GREEK PROVERB

WE MAKE A LIVING BY WHAT WE GET, BUT WE MAKE A LIFE BY WHAT WE GIVE. ♥ Winston Churchill

My gift is my song, this song's for you. ♥ ♥Elton John

I'm not afraid to look like an idiot. ♥ Anthony Bourdain

SUCCESS MAKES YOU RIDICULOUS; YOU END UP WEARING NIGHTGOWNS TO DINNER. ♥ NATALIE GOLDBERG

I long to accomplish a great and noble task, but it is my chief duty to accomplish small tasks as if they were great and noble. ♥Helen Keller

I've got the keys to my castle in the air but whether I can unlock the door remains to be seen. ♥Louisa May Alcott

There is only one You.

A MISTAKE IS SIMPLY ANOTHER WAY OF DOING THINGS. ♥ Katharine Graham

I DON'T WANT TO MAKE MONEY, I JUST WANT TO BE WONDERFUL. ♥ Marilyn Monroe AND SO SHE WAS.

You are still finding out who you are when you're in your 20s, you're just discovering your interests. For example, perhaps a quote book becomes your passion, or you touch a piano and find nirvana — it could be anything ... trains, cooking, fashion, dogs, science, woodworking, embroidery, even a country not your own. As these different interests attach themselves to you, the you you are meant to be materializes, becomes truer, deeper; life becomes more meaningful.

You have to be patient. Forty is when everything changes. Becoming your full self takes a lifetime. ♥ *Susan Branch*

You don't have to look for passion, be curious about life & it will find you. ♥ Susan Branch❀

Discipline gives wings ♥SB

WITHOUT DISCIPLINE, THERE'S NO LIFE AT ALL. ♥ *Katharine Hepburn*

SOME PEOPLE REGARD DISCIPLINE AS A CHORE. FOR ME, IT IS A KIND OF ORDER THAT SETS ME FREE TO FLY. ♥ *Julie Andrews*

We are the hero of our own story. ♥*Mary McCarthy*

I never did a day's work in my life. It was all fun. ♥Thomas Edison

I believe in the end, beauty will save the world. ♥ *Dostoevsky*

Life is either a great adventure or nothing. ♥Helen Keller

It's a dog-eat-dog world and I'm wearing Milkbone underwear.
♥ Norm on Cheers

CELEBRATE SUCCESS

We are all enriched by human endeavor. It sets a new standard, gives us a shinier star to reach for & makes us all feel just a little bit braver. ♥SB

Be sure to applaud accomplishment, for your family, your friends, your children, & don't forget YOU! Be proud, frame those awards, crack that champagne —someone has worked hard & deserves a party! ♥ SBranch

A slowness to applaud betrays the cold temper of an envious spirit. ♥ Hannah More

Quirkiness! Should be encouraged for world charm. ♥SB

Small successes, like having your poem printed in your grammar-school newspaper, or baking your first pie, give confidence and often lead to bigger successes. ♥ SUSAN BRANCH

Generosity is free. There's always more where that came from. ♥Susan Branch

Yearning to be better, to be more, to give more, to create more, to touch more hearts, to be a Valentine for the World.
♥ Susan Branch

Follow your heart.

Obstacles are those frightful things you see when you take your eyes off the goal. ♥Hannah More

HAVE ENOUGH MONEY TO LAST ME THE REST OF MY LIFE, AS LONG AS I DON'T BUY ANYTHING. ♥ Anon.

I don't know much about being a millionaire, but I bet I'd be darling at it. ♥ Dorothy Parker

Now the fair Goddess, Fortune, fall deep in Love with thee... ♥ William Shakespeare

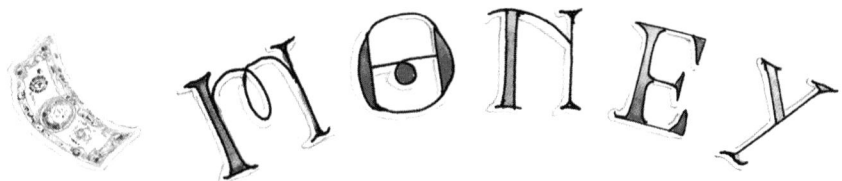

MONEY

The Greeks had just one word for "economize." Our New England grandmothers had twelve: "Eat it up, use it up, make it do, or do without."
♥ Helen Adamson

There is a gigantic difference between earning a great deal of money & being rich.
♥ Marlene Dietrich

I think everybody should get rich and famous and do everything they ever dreamed of so they can see that it's not the answer. ♥ Jim Carrey

THRIFT IS A GREAT VIRTUE ESPECIALLY WHEN IT IS PRACTICED BY OUR ANCESTORS. ♥ JOHN F. KENNEDY

It is perhaps a more fortunate destiny to have a taste for collecting shells than to be born a millionaire.
♥ Robert Louis Stevenson

Put all your eggs in one basket and
—WATCH THAT BASKET.
(The adorable) Mark Twain ♥

MATERIAL GIRLS

IF YOUR OUTGO EXCEEDS YOUR INCOME,
YOUR UPKEEP WILL BE YOUR DOWNFALL.
♥ Anon.

An alternative to Quilting Bees are Investment Clubs ~ where people get together to learn about finance and investing. As more women gain control of their own money (& therefore their own destinies), they are realizing that besides ensuring personal independence, money is a primary weapon for fighting injustice.

Money, like power, can be a devil or an angel & it all depends on who holds the purse strings & what they value. You are never too young or too old to learn about money.

Socially Responsible Investing

There are pro-fitable mutual funds that invest only in companies that are good for the earth & for people. The stocks in these funds are thoroughly researched so investors can be assured they are not supporting nuclear proliferation, polluters, tobacco, companies with poor records on equal opportunity, or companies that rely on child labor.

With our dollars we can support good things; protect the earth, defend women & children, & change the world.
♥ Susan Branch

Money doesn't grow on trees. ♥ My mom

"Are we rich?" I asked my mom. "Not rich in money," she said, "but rich in love. We have each other. That's what counts." It was a highly satisfactory answer. It sounded exactly like "Yes."

Money often costs too much. Ralph Waldo Emerson

Contentment is natural wealth. ♥ Socrates

If you lend money, think of it as giving it away, never to be seen again. If you can't do that, then don't lend it. That way, if you get it back, you'll be pleasantly surprised, and if you don't, you won't be disappointed, or worse, lose a friend over stupid money. A win-win. SB

Money may not buy happiness, but I'd rather cry in a Jaguar than on a bus. ♥ Francois Sagan

I LIKE TO SEE A MAN PROUD OF THE PLACE IN WHICH HE LIVES. I LIKE TO SEE A MAN LIVE SO HIS PLACE WILL BE PROUD OF HIM. ♥ Abraham Lincoln

Only when the last tree has died, and the last river has been poisoned and the last fish has been caught will we realize we cannot eat money. ♥ Cree Indian proverb

If nature has made you a giver, your hands are born open, and so is your heart. ♥ FRANCES HODGSON BURNETT

A toast to my brother George—the richest man in town. ♥
It's a Wonderful Life

Teach us delight  in simple things. ♥ Rudyard Kipling

Ten years ago the deficit on my farm was about a hundred dollars; but by well-designed capital expenditure, by drainage & by greater attention to details, I have got it into the thousands. ♥ Stephen Leacock

To be clever enough to get all that money, one must be dull enough to want it. ♥ G. K. Chesterton

I DON'T LIKE MONEY, ACTUALLY, BUT IT QUIETS MY NERVES. ♥ Joe Lewis

Greed is not a financial issue. It's a heart issue. ♥ ANDY STANLEY

 There must be more to life than having everything. ♥ Maurice Sendak

George Bernard Shaw's definition of a gentleman:
A man, but more often a woman, who owes
nothing & leaves the world in debt to him. ♥

You ask about funds — at present I have
8¢ in the bank, $10 owing me, & a
fortune in prospect. ♥ Louisa May Alcott

You can only become truly accomplished at something you love.
Don't make money your goal. Instead, pursue the things
you love doing, and then do them so well that people can't
take their eyes off you. ♥ Maya Angelou

If you want to know what God thinks of money, just
look at the people He gave it to. ♥ Dorothy Parker

Debt erases freedom more
surely than anything else.
♥ Merryn Somerset Webb

I rob banks because
that's where
the money is.
♥ Willie Sutton

I figure my chances of winning the lottery are the same
whether I play or not. ♥ Fran Lebowitz

Money can buy you a fine dog,
but only love can make it wag its tail.
♥ Richard Friedman

I LOVE YOU

Second grade, I colored "birds in love" for Mother's Day. ♥SB

A child her wayward pencil drew
On margins of her book;
Garlands of flowers, dancing elves,
Bud, butterfly and brook,
Lessons undone, and plumb forgot,
Seeking with hand & heart
The teacher whom she learned to love
Before she knew, 'twas art.

Louisa May Alcott

CREATIVITY

I SAW THE ANGEL IN THE MARBLE & CARVED UNTIL I SET HIM FREE. ♥ *Michelangelo*

Creativity is really the structuring of magic. ♥ ANNE KENT RUSH

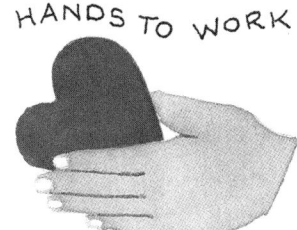

HANDS TO WORK

HEARTS TO GOD

MILLIONS LONG FOR IMMORTALITY BUT DON'T KNOW WHAT TO DO ON A RAINY AFTERNOON. ♥ SUSAN ERTZ

Magic is always pushing & drawing & making things out of nothing. ♥ Frances Hodgson Burnett

Thank goodness I was never sent to school; it would have rubbed off some of the originality BEATRIX POTTER.

IN THE MIDDLE AGES, EVERY CRAFTSMAN WAS AN ARTIST. ♥ Wm. Morris

RED CRAYON

"THERE AIN'T NO RULES AROUND HERE," said *Thomas Edison*, "WE'RE TRYING TO ACCOMPLISH SOMETHING."

IMAGINATION is the main weapon in the WAR against reality. ♥ C.S. Lewis

And when the world seems to be falling apart around you, create something, put a flower in a vase, bake a pie, draw a picture, knit socks. ♥ Susan Branch

Nothing feeds the center of being so much as creative work. The curtain of mechanization has come down between the mind & the hand. ♥ Anne Morrow Lindbergh

Neglect not the gift that is in thee. ♥ I TIMOTHY 4:14

Somebody's boring me. I think it's me. ♥ Dylan Thomas

History has remembered the kings & warriors because they destroyed; art has remembered the people because they created. ♥ Wm. Morris

If you do it with heart That's art! ♥ SB

You can't sit around and wait for somebody to say who you are. You need to write it and paint it, and do it yourself. ♥ Faith Ringgold

I am a pencil in the hand of God.
♥ MOTHER TERESA

Let yourself be
silently drawn
by the strange pull
of what you really
love; it will not
lead you astray.
♥ Rumi 1207-1273

There are two ways of spreading light: to be
the candle or the mirror that reflects it.
♥ Edith Wharton

The chief ingredient for
Inspiration is Curiosity.
SB

There are no guarantees
except one: Nothing
happens unless you try.
♥ Susan Branch

MAKING MAGIC

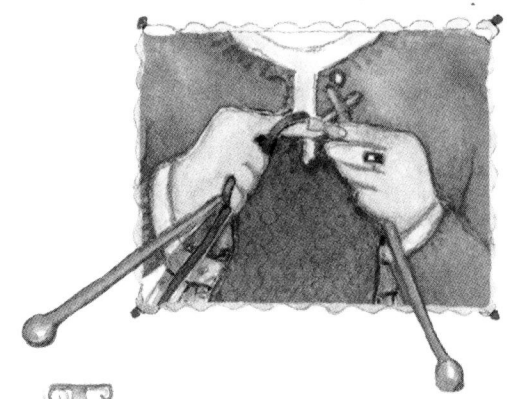

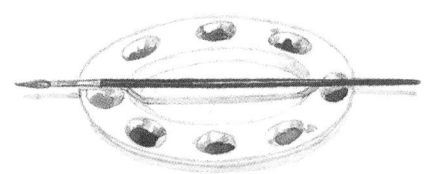

There's surely a connection between the heart & hand & it shows in homemade things ~ it's what makes them unique. ♥ SUSAN BRANCH

Her imagination was by habit ridiculously active; when the door was not open it jumped out the window.
Henry James

The solitude of a quiet life stimulates the creative mind.
♥ Albert Einstein

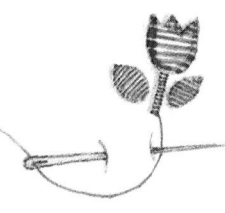

Remember the beauty you believed in as a child & use it as your muse. ♥ S.B.

Take time to just think; let it be cloaked in a daydream. Let it feel a little bit lonely.
♥ Susan Branch

If you're always trying to be normal you'll never know how amazing you can be.
♥ Maya Angelou

There is only one You.

Your work is to discover your work & then, with all your heart, give yourself to it. ♥ Buddha

Great art is as irrational as great music. It is mad with its own loveliness.
♥ George Jean Nathan

The worst enemy to creativity is self-doubt.
♥ Sylvia Plath

There is surely a piece of divinity in us, something that was born before the elements & owes no homage to the sun. ♥ Sir Thomas Browne

I dream of painting and then I paint my dream.
♥ Vincent Van Gogh

Indulge your imagination in every possible flight.
J a n e   A u s t e n

Creativity is contagious. Pass it on. ♥ Albert Einstein

Raven hair, ruby lips . . . Sparks fly from her fingertips . . .
💜 Don Henley

No, I prefer to sit here. There's so much
more scope for the imagination.
💜 L.M. Montgomery

Even in her childhood she extracted from life double
enjoyment that comes usually only to the creative
mind. "Now I am doing this. Now I am doing that,"
she told herself while she was doing it. Looking on
while she participated. 💜 Edna Ferber

Perhaps the best thing we can do for the
creative person is stay out of her way.
💜 Judith Groch

As many different noses as there are in the world, that's
how many ways there are of saying or doing the same
thing. Don't worry about being original, you already are.
💜 Susan Branch

God sent His singers upon the earth, with
songs of sadness & of mirth, that they might
touch the hearts of men, & bring them back
to heaven again. Henry Wadsworth Longfellow

I've forgiven myself for not being Beethoven. 💜 Neil Diamond

The Best New Room in the House
Creativity is really the structuring of magic.
♥ ANNE KENT RUSH

So make a "magic room" ~ a craft room. Have wide surfaces to work on, a place to keep wrapping paper & ribbon ~ organize things so you can get to them, according to your interests ~ stickers, scrapbooks, glue, glitter, colored pencils, pinking shears, hole punch, construction paper, rubber stamps, journals, stationery, fabric, yarn, ribbons, buttons, watercolors, how-to books, the sewing machine & files for collecting ideas. Decorate with your own collections ~ have music & a good chair for dreaming in. ♥

The imagination needs moodling, ~ long, inefficient, happy idling, dawdling and puttering.
♥ Brenda Ueland

Choose nothing less. WHAT MATTERS MOST, "I DID MY BEST." ♥ SB

Creativity takes courage. ♥ Henri Matisse

"THE FIRST THING YOU MUST DO," SAID THE FAIRY, "IS TO GO BACK INTO THE SITTING ROOM AND FIND MY MAGIC WAND. I'M USELESS WITHOUT IT." ♥ H.E. TODD

She cure for boredom is curiosity. There is no cure for curiosity. ♥ Dorothy Parker

H♥ME SWEET H♥ME IS H♥MEMADE! ♥ SB.

Creativity is the power to connect the unconnected. ♥ William Pollard

There are some days when I think I'm going to die from an overdose of satisfaction. ♥ Salvador Dali

I don't want to make money. I just want to be wonderful. ♥ Marilyn Monroe

The one thing that you have that nobody else has is you. Your voice, your mind, your story, your vision. So write and draw and build and play and dance and live as only you can. ♥ Neil Gaiman

The Quest for Inspiration often leads to the door of Serendipity. It's good to wake up in the morning, stretch & yawn and ask yourself (because you really don't know), "What shall we do today?" ♥ Susan Branch

We come spinning out of nothingness, scattering stars like dust. ♥ Rumi

Every artist was first an amateur. ♥ Ralph Waldo Emerson

Take time to notice the Quiet ~ stillness is the petri dish of Creativity. ♥ SB

EVERYONE GUESSES. CREATING IS NOT A SCIENCE; IT'S EXPLORING THE UNKNOWN BY YOURSELF WITHOUT A ROAD MAP. ♥ Susan Branch

CREATIVITY

We are the music makers,
and we are the dreamers
    of dreams,
Wandering by lone
    sea breakers,
And sitting by desolate
    streams;
World-losers and
    world-forsakers
On whom the pale moon
    gleams:
Yet we are the movers
    and shakers
Of the world for ever,
    it seems. ♥ "Ode" 1874 ★
        Arthur O'Shaughnessy

I read somewhere that the word "inspiration" derives from the Latin "sanctus espiritus," which means "the breath of God." Breath of God: A lovely thought all by itself ⁓ it makes perfect sense to have Providence whispering in your ear; otherwise there's too much left unexplained. ♥ Susan Branch

It's not what the world holds for you. It is what you bring to it. ♡ L.M. Montgomery

When there is an original sound in the world, it makes a hundred echoes. ♥ JOHN SHEDD

My mom said yes to every creative thing we wanted to do ~ and to everything she didn't think would kill us. ♥ S.B.

The world calls them its singers and poets and artists and storytellers; but they are just people who have never forgotten the way to fairyland. ♥L. M. Montgomery

You were born a creator. You have the power to shape your world.
♥ S.B.

Perfectionism is the voice of the oppressor, the enemy of the people. It will keep you cramped and insane your whole life. ♥Anne Lamott

We are all enriched by human endeavor. It sets a new standard, gives us a shinier star to reach for & makes us all feel just a little bit braver.
♥SB

JUST SLEEP ON IT

People like you and I, though mortal of course, like everyone else, do not grow old no matter how long we live. We never cease to stand like curious children before the great mystery into which we were born. ♥Albert Einstein

JUST MY IMAGINATION

Our talents are the gift that God gave us . . . What we make of them is our gift back to God. ♥ Leo Buscaglia

I've always thought my kindergarten art explained something profound about the two sides of my brain, but I was never sure what. Love the clouds though.

The artist is nothing without the gift, but the gift is nothing without work. ♥ Emile Zola

Talent is a wonderful thing, but it won't carry a quitter. ♥ Stephen King

Where words fail, music speaks. ♥ HANS CHRISTIAN ANDERSEN

I believe I learned my songs from the birds of the Brazilian forest. ♥ Antonio Carlos Jobim

THE ONLY THING BETTER THAN SINGING IS MORE SINGING. ♥ Ella Fitzgerald

Dancing is the poetry of the foot. ♥ John Dryden

ABCDEFGHIJKLMNOP

LOVE

My very first art was writing my name ~ hunched over paper, fist wrapped around a crayon deep in concentration. My mom was so proud, she showed it to my Dad, she taped it to the fridge. I couldn't wait to do more!

For young children, there is no difference between art and early writing skills. Copying letters and numbers is just the same as drawing a house or a flower. Making an S is hard! We discover the magic of letters making words! But more importantly, handwriting is a gateway to all kinds of creativity, it's making something from nothing. It's self-sufficiency. Subconsciously, we learn about the heart-brain-hand connection. The thrill of realizing the link between our hands, the crayon, and the mark on the paper. The power! Imagine taking the crayon away and handing a child a keyboard. So, from one artist to another, high on the soapbox of love, I say don't let it happen! Yes on cursive. Yes on pencils, pens, markers, and paint brushes!
♥ SBranch

Original is more interesting than perfect. ♥
Susan Branch

If I don't practice for a day, I know it. If I don't practice for two days, the critics know it. And if I don't practice for three days, the public knows it.
❤ Louis Armstrong

Out of the strain of the Doing, Into the peace of the Done.
❤ Julia Woodruff

My gift is my song, this song's for you. ❤
❤ Elton John

Creativity is more than the invention of original paintings, music, fashion, architecture, movies, and books. It's also in the simple ordinary arts we practice everyday, when we plant a garden, put a wreath on the door, set a pretty table, try a new recipe, make a family scrapbook, or put wild-flowers in a jar. No one can say, "I'm not creative." We create our lives everyday.
❤ Susan Branch

Nobody ever told me about this thing called "process" till I read the Autobiography of Mark Twain & HE told me! So, all this time, when I was fretting & worrying because I didn't have the answer to a problem, or idea, or something — I didn't know what to do. I was extremely impatient with myself. It got worse & worse till I figured out that this waiting period was part of the process & actually the foundation for the creation! Sometimes it seems to take FOREVER, but now I know I'm "working on it" even when I don't feel like I am! I trust that my inner self HAS the answer & will, in good time, give it to the outer me so I can GET ON WITH MY LIFE! ❤ SB

Remember

'TO EVERY THING THERE IS A SEASON AND A TIME TO EVERY PURPOSE UNDER HEAVEN

How to Draw

Drawing is a lot easier than you might think. I got a late start in drawing & painting because I never tried & I never imagined I could do it. I finally painted my first picture at age 30 — what a happy & completely unexpected surprise that was! Up till then my creative outlets were sewing, embroidery & cooking — I got an A in 7th grade art, but it was an elective & I thought everybody got an A! Confidence & belief in yourself is everything I've learned since then. After all, some people can draw — why shouldn't one of them be you?

So here's how to start : get a little drawing pad, a sharp #2 pencil, a soft eraser & a pencil sharpener. Put something in front of you that you like — I started with a potted geranium. Choose a place on your subject to begin. Use your eyes to measure distances between different points. For a pot you can start by drawing a guideline down the middle of the page & do your best to make everything on both sides of the line equal. (Feel free to erase profusely.) You can use your finger to smear the pencil to make shadows.

Try it, you might like it, and you do get better as you go along! What I loved most was getting all this "free" artwork for my walls! No-thing has to be perfect; if you can draw, you can paint — color is fun & being creative is good for the soul. ♥

♥ Susan Branch

Creativity

Get the book THE ARTIST'S WAY & open up your creative side.

Some censuring readers will scornfully say. "Why hath this lady writ her own life? Since no one cares to know whose daughter she was or whose wife she is, or how she was bred, or how she lived, or what humor or disposition she was of?"

I answer that it is true, that 'tis to no purpose to the readers, but it is to the Authoress, because I write it for my own sake, not theirs.

♥ Margaret Cavendish 1655

Preserve your memories, keep them well, what you forget you can never retell.

♥ Louisa May Alcott

KEEP A DIARY

HOW TO WRITE A DIARY

1. To begin, begin. 💜

2. Put in the date, day of the week, time of day & where you are, your view...

3. A diary does not have to be pretty.. PRIVATE!

4. Because it's only for you. KEEPOUT

5. Just say what you're thinking & tell what happened today.

6. Write about what you e wear, hear, see, feel, wan

touch, need, fear, & love.

7. Play "What if I..?" And include your hopes & dreams.

8. Add photos, fortunes, dried flowers, bird feathers, stickers, horoscopes, and words to favorite songs, poems, or quotes. Tuck in a lock of your hair, letters, recipes, ticket stubs & birthday cards.

If you dream it
You can make it so. 💜

It's not that I belong to the past, but that the past belongs to me. 💜 Mary Antin

There are places I'll remember all my life... 💜 John Lennon

I NEVER TRAVEL WITHOUT MY DIARY. ONE SHOULD ALWAYS HAVE SOMETHING SENSATIONAL TO READ ON THE TRAIN.
💜 OSCAR WILDE

I just wrote everything down...

💜 S.B.

To Love one's self is the beginning of a life-long romance. ♥ *Oscar Wilde*

Indeed I had not much wit, yet I was not an idiot ~ my wit was according to my years. ♥ *Margaret Cavendish*

AND SO IT WAS

JOURNAL ♥

Dec. 20, 1979
See you later bookie~poo~ If anyone ever tries to read you, SCREAM! ♥ SB

SPILLING YOUR GUTS IS EXACTLY AS CHARMING AS IT SOUNDS. *Fran Lebowitz*

Think only of the past as its remembrance gives you pleasure. ♥ *Jane Austen*

Keeping a diary isn't for everyone. But pouring out thoughts and ideas helped me discover who I was, everything I believed, and everything I felt. ♥ *Susan Branch*

Tell Me Your Story

MY JOURNAL

Dear Diary

December 26, 1957

This is my brand new diary, I got it for Christmas. It is the property of Susan Anne Stewart who is 10½ years old and lives on Claire Avenue in Reseda, California. If you are not me and you are reading this, you are in big trouble. If you broke the lock I will tell Mom. Put it down right now.

Mom says a diary is a place to keep secrets. Here's one, I told Karen, but that's all — a chain is the best lager for hopscotch. Try to use a rock and it will bounce.

Sue Stewart

If a child would like to grow up to be a writer, they should read their hearts out, and never go anywhere without a book, a notepad, and a diary. ❤ SBranch

can shake off everything as I write, my sorrows disappear, my courage is reborn. ♥ Anne Frank

You'd like to be a writer? Keep a journal. Without trying, over time, you'll naturally come to write in your own voice. Like your mom told you, "Just be yourself."
Susan Branch

Journaling proves to you that you can handle anything. ♥ SUSAN BRANCH

f you want to write, you need to keep an honest unpublishable diary that nobody reads ~ nobody but you. ♥ Madeleine L'Engle

Writing in a diary is a really strange experience for someone like me. Not only because I've never written anything before, but also because it seems to me that later on neither I nor anyone else will be interested in the musings of a thirteen-year-old schoolgirl.
♥ Anne Frank

KEEP A DIARY, and SOMEDAY IT WILL KEEP YOU. ♥ Mae West

No one is reading my diary, that's for sure!
♥ ERIN DUFFY

The starting point of discovering your gifts, your talents, your dreams, is being comfortable with yourself. Spend time alone. Write in a journal. ♥ Robin Sharma

Fill your paper with the breathings of your heart.
♥ Wm. Wordsworth

We do not remember days, we remember moments. ♥ CESARE PAVESE

I always kept two books in my pocket, one to read, and one to write in.
♥ Robert Louis Stevenson

My bursting heart must find vent at my pen.
♥ Abigail Adams

The mediator between the brain & the hands must be the heart.
♥ 1927 Metropolis

DEAR DIARY

God has given us our memories that we might have roses in December.
♥ J. M. Barrie

A diary means yes indeed.
♥ Gertrude Stein

Writing things down gives focus to days. ♥ SB

Take care of all your memories, for you cannot relive them. ♥ Bob Dylan

Regular writing lifts self-esteem, helps achieve goals, & relieves stress. It's a wonderful place to count your blessings: Every day write down 3 things you love. Imagine what your books will mean to you years from now. Just write like you talk ~

that's your true voice. 🖤

🖤 SUSAN BRANCH

My Life

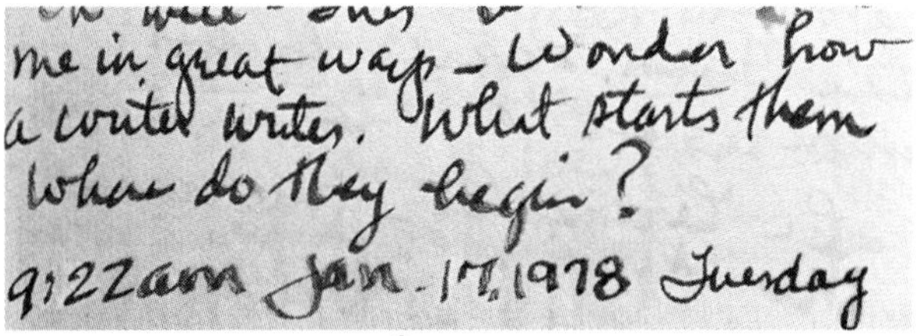

me in great way — Wonder how
a writer writes. What starts them
where do they begin?
9:22am Jan. 17, 1978 Tuesday

From my diary

FIRST WONDER

GOES DEEPEST.
♥ Yann Martel

There are many little ways
to enlarge your child's world—
love of books is best of all.
♥ Jacqueline Kennedy

Books

What a blessing it is to love books. Everybody must love something, & I know of no objects of love that give such substantial & unfailing returns as books & a garden. ♥ Elizabeth von Arnim

Then it was that books began to happen to me, and I began to believe in nothing but books and the wonderful world in books. ♥ Langston Hughes

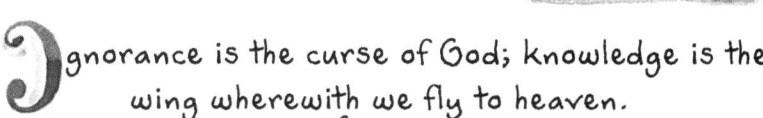

My passion for books has changed my life. ♥ Marley Dias

A book lying idle on a shelf is wasted ammunition. ♥ Henry Miller

Ignorance is the curse of God; knowledge is the wing wherewith we fly to heaven. ♥ William Shakespeare

Isn't it splendid to think of all the things there are to find out about? It makes me glad to be alive ~ it's such an interesting world. It wouldn't be half so interesting if we knew all about everything, would it? There'd be no scope for imagination then, would there? ♥ L. M. Montgomery, Anne of Green Gables

Oh for a book and a shady nook, either in door or out.

♥ JOHN WILSON

The world was hers
for the reading.
♥ Betty Smith

BEATRIX POTTER'S DIARY

Secret Garden

AUTOBIOGRAPHY OF
MARK TWAIN

Reading is
dreaming
while
wide awake.
♥ Author Unknown

The beautiful thing about learning is that
no one can take it away from you.
B. B. King

How am I to sing your praise, Happy chimney-corner days,
Sitting safe in nursery nooks, Reading picture story-books.
♥ Robert Lewis Stevenson

WE READ TO KNOW
WE'RE NOT ALONE.
♥ C.S. Lewis

I'm a product of endless books.
C. S. Lewis

There is more treasure in books than in all the pirate's loot
on Treasure Island. ♥ Walt Disney

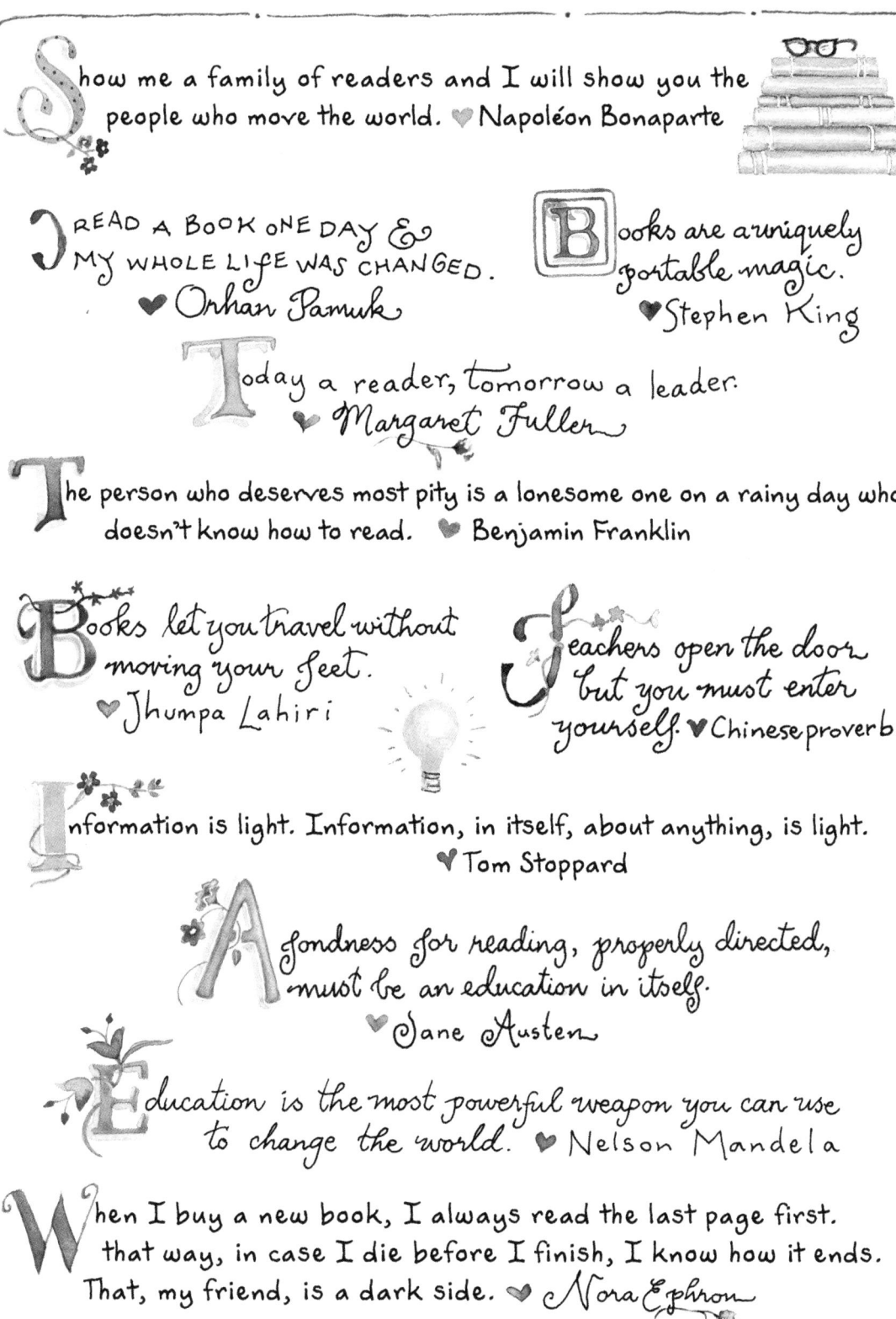

Show me a family of readers and I will show you the people who move the world. ♥ Napoléon Bonaparte

I READ A BOOK ONE DAY & MY WHOLE LIFE WAS CHANGED. ♥ Orhan Pamuk

Books are a uniquely portable magic. ♥ Stephen King

Today a reader, tomorrow a leader. ♥ Margaret Fuller

The person who deserves most pity is a lonesome one on a rainy day who doesn't know how to read. ♥ Benjamin Franklin

Books let you travel without moving your feet. ♥ Jhumpa Lahiri

Teachers open the door but you must enter yourself. ♥ Chinese proverb

Information is light. Information, in itself, about anything, is light. ♥ Tom Stoppard

A fondness for reading, properly directed, must be an education in itself. ♥ Jane Austen

Education is the most powerful weapon you can use to change the world. ♥ Nelson Mandela

When I buy a new book, I always read the last page first. that way, in case I die before I finish, I know how it ends. That, my friend, is a dark side. ♥ Nora Ephron

She is too fond of books, & it has turned her brain. ♥ Louisa May Alcott

I read a book the other day. All about civilization or something. A nutty kind of a book.
♥ Jean Harlow in DINNER AT EIGHT

DISPLAY OLD BOOKS; FAVORITES FROM YOUR CHILDHOOD; BOOKS BY YOUR HEROES. ♥ SB

I love books that make me cry. ♥ S.B.

She had always been an unashamed reader of novels.
♥ Barbara Pym

You can never get a cup of tea large enough or a book long enough to suit me—
♥ C.S. LEWIS

I love the smell of book ink in the morning.
Umberto Eco

"MARRY ME, MY WONDERFUL DARLING FRIEND,"
Mr. Knightley says to Emma in the orchard (as I sob underneath my blanket).
♥ SB

My Diary
Heroes
COOKING
COTTAGE GARDENS
FUN WITH COMPUTER
LetteRing
Making Stuff
Watercolors
Quilting
DECORATING
Creative Writing

Books break the shackles of time. ♥ Carl Sagan

Feed your Head. ♥ Grace Slick

Want to be a writer? Read, read, read. Read everything~ trash, classics, good and bad, and see how they do it. Just like a carpenter who works as an apprentice and studies the master. Read! You'll absorb it. Then write. If it's good you'll find out. If it's not, throw it out and start over. ♥ after William Faulkner

Education is simply the soul of a society as it passes from one generation to another.
♥ G. K. Chesterton

The highest result of education is tolerance. ♥ Helen Keller

What an astonishing thing a book is . . . one glance at it and you're inside the mind of another person, maybe somebody dead for thousands of years. Across the millennia an author is speaking clearly and silently inside your head, directly to you. Magic. ♥ Carl Sagan

Books give a soul to the universe, wings to the mind, flight to the imagination, & life to everything.
♥ Plato

Knowledge is the prime need of the hour.
♥ Mary McLeod Bethune

Where they burn books, at the end, they also burn people.
♥ Heinrich Heine

155

The whole world opened to me when I learned to read.
♥ Mary McLeod Bethune

Socrates said that all knowledge is possessed by the soul and it's just a matter of remembering it. Which is why we read a book and think, "I could have written that. That is so me!"
♥ Susan Branch

The world of books is still the world.
♥ ELIZABETH BARRETT BROWNING

In a good bookroom you feel that in some mysterious way you are absorbing the wisdom contained in all the books through your skin without even opening them. ♥ Mark Twain

The reader who is illuminated is, in a real sense, the poem.
♥ H. M. Tomlinson

The reading of good books is like a conversation with the finest minds of the past centuries.
♥ René Descartes

Knowledge is love & light & vision.
♥ Helen Keller

Books and doors are the same thing. You open them, and you go into another world. ♥ Jeanette Winterson

The greatest part of a writer's time is spent in reading. In order to write, a man will turn over half a library to make one book. ♥ Samuel Johnson

Black girl stories are not just for Black girls; they're for everybody. ♥ Marley Dias

Think before you speak. Read before you think. ♥ Fran Lebowitz

If you don't know history, then you don't know anything. You are a leaf that doesn't know it is part of a tree. ♥ Michael Crichton

The past is a foreign country. They do things differently there. ♥ L. P. Hartley

The only end of writing is to enable readers better to enjoy life, or better to endure it. ♥ Samuel Johnson

If there's a book that you want to read, but it hasn't been written yet, then you must write it. ♥ Toni Morrison

LIBRARY DAYS

The public library became a haven to me on hot summer days when I was about 8 or 9 — I spent a good part of every summer luxuriating in the air-conditioned quiet there. The library was only a couple of blocks from my house so I walked there, barefoot & I remember how wonderful that cold, smooth floor felt on my hot little feet. I remember the way the library smelled — that good book smell & I remember walking home with my arms overflowing with romance, adventure, fantasy & inspiration. I adored fairy tales, _The Red Book of Fairy Tales_, _The Yellow Book of Fairy Tales_, every book of fairy tales. I loved books about big families like mine, _The All of a Kind Family_ series was my favorite. When I was 15 I read _Gone With the Wind_ & sobbed into my pillow at the end. I still have a copy of that sweet story _Seventeenth Summer_ just for the feeling of that time of my life. Summer & books go hand-in-hand in my mind. I read on the porch swing, I read in a tree (I learned about reading in a tree from a book, of course). I read in my "secret place" (another book), I read at the beach, in the bathtub, in my bed, with my bologna sandwich, at the park & in the car. These days my favorite thing is to take my book & go out to lunch. I love finding things in old books so now I decorate the books I like best with a flower to dry between the pages; a leftover piece of artwork to use as a bookmark; or cartoons I think are funny — so someday in the future someone will find my little things & wonder about the person who put them there. Me! ♥

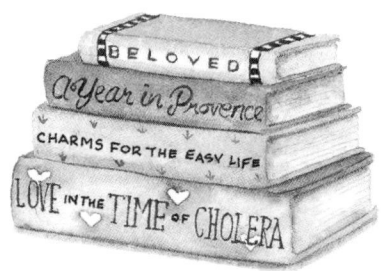

I owe everything to the
Reseda Public Library,

Susan Branch

158

If they don't educate you, then you'll have to do it yourself. ♥ S.B.

What one loves in childhood stays in the heart forever. ♥
MARY JO PUTNEY

She tried to act as though it were nothing to go to the library alone. But her happiness betrayed her. Her smile could not be restrained, and it spread from her tightly pressed mouth, to her round cheeks, almost to the hair ribbons tied in perky bows over her ears. ♥ *Maud Hart Lovelace*

The game was to just find Something about everything to be Glad about no matter what 'twas... You see, when you're hunting for the Glad things you sort of forget the other kind. ♥

Eleanor Porter, Pollyanna

Life-changing information for a 9-year-old. *Susan Branch*

159

Read a Good Little Book
I've loved these:

Enchanted April (von Arnim),
Charms for the Easy Life
(Gibbons), Like Water for
Chocolate (Esquivel), Accidental
Tourist (Tyler), The Autobiogra-
phy of Ben Franklin, Mayflower
(Philbrick), Rebecca (du Maurier),
A Gentleman in Moscow (Towles).
Autobiography of Mark Twain,
All Creatures Great and Small
(Herriot), Howard's End (Forster),
Forgotten Garden (Morton),
Zelda (Milford), Einstein's
Dreams (Lightman) ♥

So labour at your Alphabet,
For by that learning
Shall you get
To lands where Fairies may
be met. ♥ *Andrew Lang*

YOU'RE NEVER TOO OLD
FOR FAIRYTALES. ♥

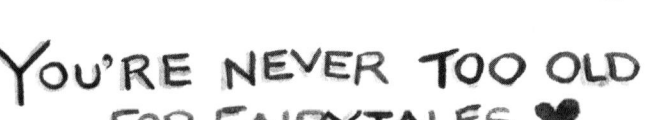

Fairy Tales

Nothing can be truer than fairy wisdom. It's as true as Sunbeams.
♥ Douglas Jerrold

The way to read a fairytale is to throw yourself in.
♥ W. H. Auden

 left the fary tales lying on the floor of the nursery, and I have not found any books so sensible since. ♥ G. K. Chesterton

A children's story that can only be enjoyed by children is not a good children's story in the slightest.
♥ C. S. Lewis

Once upon a time

Choose happily-ever-after, anything else won't do.
♥ S.B.

So come with me where dreams are born & time is never planned.
J. M. Barrie

Little Red Riding Hood was my first love. I felt that if I could have married Little Red Riding Hood, I should have known happiness.
CHARLES DICKENS

Life itself is the most wonderful fairy tale of all.
♥ Hans Christian Andersen

Everything was romantic in my imagination. The woods were peopled by the mysterious good folk. ♥ Beatrix Potter

The fairies, as was their custom, clapped their hands with delight over their cleverness.
J. M. Barrie

Everyone's life is a fairy tale written by God's fingers.
♥ Hans Christian Andersen

Every child can remember laying his head in the grass, staring into the infinitesimal forest & seeing it grow populous with fairy armies. ROBT. LOUIS STEVENSON

Now & then, in this workaday world, things do happen in the delightful storybook fashion, & what a comfort that is.
Louisa May Alcott

There's no reason why facts can't be fairytales & fairytales, facts. ♥ SB

A safe fairyland is unknown in all worlds. ♥ J.R.R. Tolkien

Children see magic because they look for it.
♥ Christopher Moore

I don't want realism!
I want magic!
Tennessee Williams

One gift the fairies gave me: (three, they commonly
bestowed of yore:) the love of books, the golden key,
That opens the enchanted door. ♥ Andrew Lang

If you want your children to be intelligent,
read them fairy tales. If
you want them to be more
intelligent, read them more
fairy tales. ♥ Albert Einstein

Children, children, don't forget
There are elves & fairies yet.
♥ Dora Owen

In a utilitarian age, of all other times,
it is a matter of grave importance that
fairy tales should be respected.
Charles Dickens

There is the great lesson of Beauty & the Beast,
that a thing must be loved before it is lovable.
♥ G.K. Chesterton

ALL THE WORLD IS MADE of FAITH & PIXIE DUST.
♥ J.M. Barrie

When they came to the little house they saw that it was built of bread & covered with cakes with windows of clear sugar.

Hansel & Gretel

GOD IS ALIVE, MAGIC IS AFOOT.
Buffy St. Marie

And then he began to play so sweetly that the poor girl stood as if *enchanted* & her heart was filled with joy. ♥ Grimm's Fairy Tales

Thy loving smile will surely hail the love gift of a fairy tale.
♥ Lewis Carroll

In the evening she came to a large forest, & she was so tired from sorrow & hunger & from the long walk that she climbed into a hollow tree & fell asleep. ♥ Brothers Grimm

And the herdsman had seen in the girl's eyes a world just like that: a world of wonder, a world not of grass & wild creatures but of human glances. A world of things that dwell in the heart. ♥ FRENCH FAIRY TALES

Unhindered she went thither & found everything as the night wind had promised. Brothers Grimm

Then Lena said to Foundling, "If you won't forsake me, I won't forsake you." "Never, ever," said Foundling. ♥ Grimm's Fairytales

Go not to the Elves for counsel, for they will say both no & yes. ♥ J.R.R. Tolkien

For the trouble with the real folk of Faerie is that they do not always look like what they are. J.R.R. Tolkien

"On the matter of brains, I can do nothing for them," said the fairy. ♥ Charles Perrault

Guardian angels don't always wear white. ♥ SB

The loveliest tinkle as of golden bells answered him. It is fairy language. You ordinary children can never hear it, but if you were to hear it, you would know that you had heard it once before. ♥ J.M. Barrie

How, without the aid of the fairy folk, could there be so little mildew in the corn? ♥ Beatrix Potter
Proof positive. ♥

Once Upon a Time

They came to a dear little room & the Prince said to Folly that henceforth this room would be reserved for her. ♥
Folly in Fairyland, Carolyn Wells

NOW IT HAPPENED THAT A PRINCE CAME TO THE FOREST ONE DAY & WHEN HE ARRIVED AT THE DWARFS' COTTAGE, HE DECIDED TO SPEND THE NIGHT. ♥ Grimm's Fairy Tales

Her cat was constantly with her, & ran after her wherever she went, and even sat up proudly by her side when she drove out in her fine glass coach. ♥ The Brown Fairy Book

Three elves came & conducted her to a hollow mountain where the little folks lived. Everything was small but more elegant & beautiful than can be described. ♥ Brothers Grimm

You, yourself,
are
the magic.
SB

Those who don't believe in magic
will never find it.

ROALD DAHL

I want to be magic. I want to touch the heart of the world
and make it smile. I want to be a friend of elves and live
in a tree. Or under a hill. I want to marry a moonbeam and hear
the stars sing. I don't want to pretend at magic anymore,
I want to be magic. ♥ Charles de Lint

Any man can lose his hat in a fairy wind.
♥ Irish Saying

Never let anyone tell you magic
doesn't exist or that fairies
aren't real. It isn't cynicism that
will change the world. ♥ SB

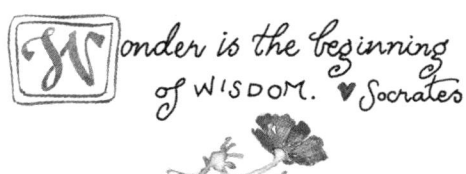

Wonder is the beginning
of WISDOM. ♥ Socrates

Where the knotty hawthorne grows,
Look for prints of fairy toes.
♥ Dora Owen

Come cuddle close in daddy's coat
beside the fire so bright,
And hear about the fairy folk
That wander in the night.
♥ Robert Bird

Fairy Tales & magic!

AUTHORHOOD

History will be kind to me for I intend to write it myself.
♡ Winston Churchill

We shall show them. We shall give them a bunny book to conjure with.

Norman Warne to Beatrix Potter in
MISS POTTER

172

WRITING & WRITERS

TIME HAS PASSED THROUGH ME & BECOME A SONG. ♥ Holly Near

You own everything that happened to you. Tell your stories. If people wanted you to write warmly about them, they should've behaved better. ♥ Anne Lamott

Don't forget ~ no one else sees the world the way you do, so no one else can tell the stories that you have to tell. ♥ Charles de Lint

WORDS LOVE, HEAL, GIVE HOPE.

"Do you know," Peter asked, "why swallows build in the eaves of houses? It's to listen to the stories." ♥ J.M. Barrie

SPOKEN WORDS ARE LOST... BUT THE WRITTEN WORD LIVES FOREVER. ♥ SB

My characters shall have, after a little trouble, all that they desire. ♥ Jane Austen

We have met the enemy and he is us. ♥ Walt Kelly

There is something delicious about writing the first words of a story. You never quite know where they'll take you. ♥ BEATRIX POTTER

BEAUTY WAS NOT SIMPLY SOMETHING TO BEHOLD; IT WAS SOMETHING ONE COULD DO.
♥ Toni Morrison

EXCELLENCE DOES NOT REQUIRE PERFECTION.
♥ Henry James

When you are describing
A shape, or sound, or tint,
Don't state the matter plainly,
But put it in a hint;
And learn to look at all things,
With a sort of mental squint.
♥ Lewis Carroll

Let other pens dwell on guilt and misery.
Jane Austen

Nor would I miss the early darkness & the pleasant firelight tea and long evenings among my books.
♥ Elizabeth von Arnim

Was Thoreau ever lonely? Certainly. Where do you think writing like his came from? Camaraderie?
♥ Jessamyn West

I like good strong words that mean something.
♥ Louisa May Alcott

If only I could write something splendid that would set other hearts on fire. ♥ Louisa May Alcott

If you be pungent, be brief, for it is with words as with sunbeams: the more they are condensed, the deeper they burn. ♥ John Dryden

*B*roadly speaking, short words are best & the old words, when short, are best of all. ♥ *Winston Churchill*

*W*ords have so much power, the power to break hearts & make war; the power to create joy & heal wounds. My favorite are the Golden Words, words of hope, words that resonate in beauty & truth, words that raise our hearts & spirits to higher levels & make us proud to be human beings. To live up to their full meaning is to reach for the stars. ✧

GENEROSITY, COURAGE, Empathy, DISCIPLINE, CHARM, GRACE, GOODNESS, INTEGRITY, BEAUTY, SPIRIT, ENTHUSIASM, JOY, HOPE, COMPASSION, FORGIVENESS, TRUTH CUROSITY, & LOVE

*A*nd remember, *Faith* can move a mountain...
♥ *Susan Branch*

*S*ticks and stones can break your bones but words can break your heart. ♥ SUSAN BRANCH

175

The best time for planning a book is while you're doing the dishes.
♥ Agatha Christie

Writing is show business for shy people.
♥ Lee Child

The blank page is God's way of letting us know how hard it is to be God. ♥ G. K. Chesterton

No tears for the writer, no tears for the reader.
♥ ROBERT FROST

The words "far far away" have always had a strange charm.
♥ Alfred Tennyson

It seems to me that on one page I recognized a portion of an old diary of mine which mysteriously disappeared shortly after my marriage, and also, scraps of letters which, though considerably edited, sound to me vaguely familiar. In fact, Mr. Fitzgerald (I believe that is how he spells his name) seems to believe that plagiarism begins at home.
♥ Zelda Fitzgerald

I wish I could write a beautiful book to break those hearts that are soon to cease to exist: a book of faith & small neat worlds & of people that live by the philosophies of popular songs.
♥ Zelda Fitzgerald

Writing should be like a cottage garden, with no straight path; it should meander, around corners, through creaking gates, looking for the secret places ~ like life.
♥ Susan Branch

I am like a blind pig when I work.
Ernest Hemingway

If you try & fail that's better than saying, I could have written if I hadn't married Harold.
♥ CAROLYN SEE

Having your book turned into a movie is like seeing your oxen turned into bouillon cubes. ♥ John LeCarré

Truth, in her dress, finds facts too tight. In fiction, she moves with ease. ♥ Rabindranath Tagore

It's none of their business that you have to learn to write. Let them think you were born that way. ♥ Ernest Hemingway

Just write every day of your life. Read intensely. Then see what happens. Most of my friends who are put on that diet have very pleasant careers. ♥ Ray Bradbury

Do not hoard what seems good for a later place in the book, or for another book: give it, give it all, give it now.
♥ Annie Dillard

Go, little book, and wish to all
Flowers in the garden, meat in the hall,
A bin of wine, a spice of wit,
A house with lawns enclosing it,
A living river by the door,
A nightingale in the sycamore!
♥ Robert Louis Stevenson ♥

Books.
Cats.
Life is
Good.
＝^..^＝ Edward Gorey

I get mail:

Someday, I want to be a writer for women like you are. I love to write. I hope you'll write me back! ♡
Love,
Ellery ♡

'Till this moment I never knew myself.
♥ Jane Austen

If a book come from the heart, it will contrive to reach other hearts. ♥ Thomas Carlyle

After that, work & hope. But never hope more than you work.
♥ Beryl Markham

When I grow up, I'm going to write for children, & grownups that haven't grown up too much, all the earthsongs I now do hear? ♥ Opal Whiteley

With freedom, books, flowers, & the moon ~ who could not be happy. ♥ Oscar Wilde

Drama is very important in life: You have to come on with a bang.
♥ Julia Child

I don't want anyone reading my writing to think about style. I just want them to be in the story. ♥ WILLA CATHER

There is no royal road to anything, it's one thing at a time, all things in succession. That which grows fast withers as rapidly. That which grows slowly, endures.
♥ Josiah Gilbert Holland

To write well, express yourself like the common people, but think like a wise man. ♥ Aristotle

WHERE SHALL I BEGIN? WHICH OF MY IMPORTANT THINGS SHALL I TELL YOU FIRST?
Jane Austen

Writing a book is like working a jigsaw puzzle that has no pieces. So, first you make the pieces. They are huge and clunky and barely fit together, but you keep working on it. There are too many holes, so you make smaller pieces. And things begin to come together. In the end the pieces are so small, they are barely visible to the eye. But those are the best. They tighten everything. They are the finishers.
♥ Susan Branch

Atticus told me to delete the adjectives & I'd have the facts. ♥ Harper Lee

Without a doubt the two best words in the English language are The End. ♥ Ken Scott

It's hell writing & it's hell not writing. The only tolerable state is having just written.
♥ Robert Hass

No price is too high to pay for the privilege of owning yourself.
♥ Rudyard Kipling

THE PURPOSE OF LITERATURE IS TO TURN BLOOD INTO INK.
♥ T.S. Eliot

With educated people, I suppose, punctuation is a matter of rule; with me it is a matter of feeling. But I must say I have great respect for the semicolon; it's a useful little chap..

♥ *Abraham Lincoln*

She had one of those small summery brains that flower early & run to seed. ♥ Dorothy Sayers

To send a letter is
a good way to go
somewhere without

moving anything but
your heart.
Phyllis Theroux

Handwritten LETTERS

with love from me to you

MORE THAN KISSES, LETTERS MINGLE SOULS. ♥ John Donne

I LOVE THE NOSTALGIC MYSELF. I HOPE WE NEVER LOSE SOME OF THE THINGS OF THE PAST. *Walt Disney*

What a wonderful thing is a letter, capable of conveying a kiss across continents.
♥ AUTHOR UNKNOWN

A handwritten, personal letter has become a genuine modern-day luxury.
♥ Shana Alexander

Your letters are always to me fresher than flowers without their fading so soon. ♥ *Lady Morgan*

ALL GOOD NEWS

Since I have no sweet flower to send you, I enclose my heart.
♥ *Emily Dickinson*

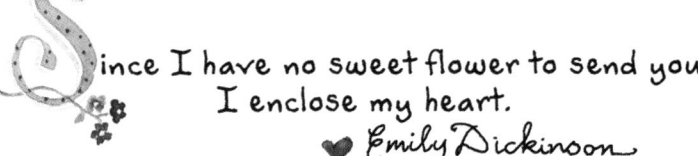

The whistling postman swings along,
His bag is deep & wide,
And messages from all the world
Are bundled up inside.
♥ *Anonymous*

I wear the key of memory & can open
every door in the house of my life.
♥ Amelia E. Barr

Always serve letters
with a cup of
tea and a footstool.
♥ MACRINA WIEDERKEHR

But letters were letters then; & we made
great prizes of them, & read them &
studied them like books. ♥ Elizabeth Gaskell

Behold me going to write you as handsome a letter as I can.
Wish me good luck. ♥ Jane Austen

A letter is like immortality. Kept forever,
they're a window into the past, a step back in time,
a connection with all that came before. Home and family
and old loves slipstitched together in eternity.
♥ SUSAN BRANCH

I thank you for such a long letter, and yet if
I might choose, the next should be longer.
I think a letter just about three-days long
would make me happier than any other
kind, if you please. ♥ Emily Dickinson

Letter writing on the part of a busy man or woman is
the quintessence of generosity. ♥ AGNES REPPLIER

On the road between the houses of friends grass does not grow.
♥ *Norwegian proverb*

And SEAL IT WITH A KISS ♥

Wild Thing, You make my heart sing — You make everything groovy ♥ *The Troggs*

Hi! Guess w

Febr

I'm so glad I lived during the last hurrah of the hand-written letter. I have a basket with a lid on it where I keep old letters — letters from my grandma (she calls me "darling"), including the last one I ever got from her; letters from my parents; love letters from old boyfriends (one with a marriage proposal); fun letters from my girlfriends & penpals; & years of correspondence from my best friend Diana. ♥ *Susan Branch*

FILL YOUR PAPER WITH THE BREATHINGS OF YOUR HEART. ♥ *William Wordsworth*

TO WRITE IS HUMAN~ TO RECEIVE A LETTER? Divine! ♥ *Susan Landroth* ♥

Back on its golden hinges The gate of memory swings ~ And my heart goes in the garden and walks with olden things. ♥ *Ella Wheeler Wilcox*

GIRL SCOUT PEN PAL BADGE

I stayed in a really old hotel last night. They sent me a wake-up letter. ♥ *Stephen Wright*

You're going
to ♥
LOVE this...

Love is the perfume that clings to old letters. ♥ Susan Branch

You deserve a longer letter than this, but it is my unhappy fate seldom to treat people so well as they deserve. ♥ Jane Austen

Across the gateway
of my heart, I wrote
'No thoroughfare'
But love came
laughing by and cried,
'I enter everywhere.'

♥ Herbert Shipman

LOVE

LOVE IS THE
IRRESISTIBLE DESIRE
TO BE DESIRED
IRRESISTIBLY.
Louis Ginsberg

At the side of the everlasting why,
is a yes, and a yes, and a yes.
E. M. Forster

To Know, Know, Know You is
to Love, Love, Love You.
Phil Spector

There's nothing half so
sweet in life as love's
young dream.
Clement C. Moore

The love in your heart
wasn't put there to stay,
Love isn't Love
till it's given away.
Saw on a pillow in the UK

Love is friendship set to music.
Anon.

LOVE

Now in a cottage built of lilacs and laughter
I know the meaning of the words "ever-after..."
Johnny Burke for Frank Sinatra

POTIONS, SPELLS, SUPERSTITIONS OF LOVE

PIN IVY TO YOUR BREAST ON NEW YEAR'S DAY – YOU WILL MARRY THE NEXT MAN/WOMAN YOU SPEAK TO. (DON'T JUST BE TALKING TO ANYBODY.) ♡

MAKE A TEA FROM HEARTSEASE. BRUSH COOL LIQUID OVER EYELIDS OF SLEEPING LOVED ONE. HE WILL LOVE THE FIRST ONE HE SEES. DRINK TEA TO CURE HEARTBREAK. ♡

BLOW ALL OF THE FEATHERY REMAINS OFF A BLOWN DANDELION FLOWER WITH ONE BREATH. YOU WILL GET YOUR WISH.

JUST BEFORE BED, HARD BOIL AN EGG, CUT IT IN HALF + DISCARD YOLK. SALT THE HALVES OF EGG. SIT ON SOMETHING YOU NEVER SAT ON BEFORE + EAT THE EGG. WALK TO BED BACKWARD. YOU WILL DREAM OF YOUR FUTURE MATE. ♡

TIE A NARROW BLUE SATIN RIBBON TO YOUR LEFT ANKLE – GO BARE-FOOT ALL DAY + YOU WILL SOON BE KISSED PROPERLY.

IF YOU FIND A SMALL SPIDER IN THE FOLDS OF YOUR WEDDING DRESS YOU WILL NEVER BE POOR. ♡

BAKE A WHOLE ALMOND INTO THE WEDDING CAKE + THE GUEST WHO FINDS IT WILL RECEIVE LONG LIFE AND PROSPERITY.

HOLD AN APPLE IN YOUR LEFT HAND, SAY "ADAM, ADAM, ADAM" 3 TIMES, BITE THE APPLE, HOLD YOUR BREATH, CHEW + SWALLOW. COMMUNICATION LINES ARE OPEN.

FAIRY DUST

HEARTSEASE

LOVE-IN-IDLENESS

TO BE FOREVER BEAUTIFUL: AT EXACTLY SUNRISE ON THE FIRST OF MAY GO OUTSIDE AND ROLL NAKED IN THE DEW. ♡

IF HE HAS BEEN UNFAITHFUL – TO GAIN YOU BACK HE MUST GATHER HAIR FROM THE FACE OF A WOLF (INCLUDING WHISKERS) – THEN BURN THEM + DRINK THE ASHES IN A SHOTGLASS FULL OF SOUR MILK. IF HE LIVES, YOU MAY FORGIVE HIM + BE CONFIDENT OF HIS FIDELITY. ♡

IF YOU CRY, CATCH YOUR TEARS IN A CUP, SPRINKLE THEM ON YOUR LOVER'S PILLOW – HE WILL EXPERI-ENCE A GREAT CHANGE OF HEART. ♡

AIR YOUR FEATHER QUILT ON A LINE THE FIRST CLEAR DAY AFTER THE VERNAL EQUINOX – PUT IT BACK ON THE BED – YOUR LOVE WILL BE REFRESHED AND RENEWED. ♡

♡ Susan Branch

Aren't you lovely in all your heart conveys.
♥ IVA ST. J - WHITMAN

WISHING & WANTING TO SEE YOU, I STEP ON THIN ICE.
♥ Madoka Mayuzumi

ROMANCE

of thee I sing... ♫

Keep rosemary by your garden gate. Add pepper to your mashed potatoes. Plant roses & lavender for luck. Fall in love whenever you can.
♥ Alice Hoffman

By the light of the silvery moon,... We'll croon love's tune~
♥ Edward Madden

WHATEVER SOULS ARE MADE of, HIS & mine ARE THE SAME. Emily Brontë

There is no exercise better for the heart than reaching out & lifting others up.
John Holmes

All that was ever ours is ours forever.
♥ Amy Carmichael

For she fears that one will ask her for eternity & she's so busy being free.
♥ Joni Mitchell

LOVE DOESN'T MAKE THE WORLD GO 'ROUND
LOVE IS WHAT MAKES THE RIDE WORTHWHILE.
♥ FRANKLIN P. JONES

Hearts that never lean, must fall. ♥ Emily Dickinson

THE VERIE INSTANT THAT I SAW
YOU, DID
MY HEART FLIE TO YOUR SERVICE.
♥ Wm. Shakespeare

WE SHOULD COUNT TIME BY HEART-THROBS.
♥ Philip Jones Bailey

The essential elements . . . of the romantic
spirit are curiosity and the love of beauty.
♥ Walter Pater ♥

DO
NOT
DISTURB

Beautiful faces are
those that wear
Whole-souled honesty
printed there.
♥ Ellen Palmer Allerton

I KNOW YOU
by heart.
♥ S.B.

You must always be awaggle with Love...
D. H. LAWRENCE

There is no charm equal to tenderness of heart.
♥ Jane Austen

WHAT IS LOVE?

LOVE IS LOVE'S REWARD. *John Dryden* ♥ LOVE IS NOT TO BE TRIFLED WITH. *French Proverb* ♥ LOVE IS A MANY SPLENDORED THING. *Paul Francis Webster* LOVE MAKES THE WORLD GO ROUND. *French Song* ♥ LOVE DOESN'T MAKE THE WORLD GO ROUND. LOVE IS WHAT MAKES THE RIDE WORTHWHILE. *Franklin P. Jones* ♥ LOVE KNOWS NO BOUNDS. *Anonymous* ♥ WHAT IS LOVE? FIVE FEET OF HEAVEN IN A PONYTAIL! *Morton & Michaels* ♥ LOVE IS BLIND. *Chaucer* ♥ LOVE IS THE ONLY GAME THAT IS NOT CALLED ON ACCOUNT OF DARKNESS. *Anonymous* ♥ LOVE IS HEAVEN AND HEAVEN IS LOVE. *Sir Walter Scott* ♥ LOVE IS THE TRIUMPH OF IMAGINATION OVER INTELLIGENCE. *H. L. Mencken* ♥ LOVE IS ALL YOU NEED. *The Beatles* ♥ LOVE IS THE THING. *Anonymous* WHAT IS LOVE? . . .

A loving heart is the truest wisdom.
♥ CHARLES DICKENS

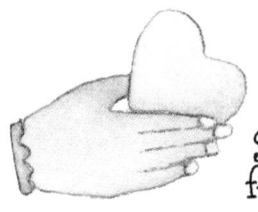

...how truly is a kind heart a fountain of gladness, making everything in its vicinity to freshen into smiles! ♥ Washington Irving

YOU ONLY NEED A HEART FULL OF GRACE, A SOUL GENERATED BY LOVE." A HEART FULL OF GRACE, A SOUL GENERATED BY LOVE. A HEART FULL OF LOVE. ♥ DR. MARTIN LUTHER KING, JR.

Every act of love is a work of peace no matter how small. ♥ Mother Teresa

You are the sunshine of my life! xx

On a windy day let's go flying
There may be no trees to rest on
There may be no clouds to ride
But we'll have our wings and the wind will be with us
That's enough for me, that's enough for me." ♥ Yoko Ono

'Stay' is a Charming word in a friend's Vocabulary
♥ Louisa May Alcott

Hours fly
flowers die
new days
new ways
Pass by
Love stays

Carved in stone
on a dovecote in the
Cotswolds ♥

A heart as soft,
a heart as kind,
A heart as sound and
free As in the whole
world thou canst find,
That heart
I'll give to thee.
Robert Herrick

Look for a sweet person. Forget rich.
♥ Estée Lauder

Before you find your soulmate, you must discover your soul.
♥ Charles F. Glassman

Where there is
great love,
There are always
miracles.
♥ Willa Cather

Valentine Toasts

She says

Here's to one and only one
And may that one be he,
Who loves but one and only one,
And may that one be me.

anon.

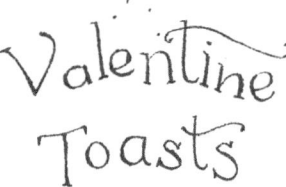

He says

Give me a kisse, and to that kisse a score;
Then to that twenty, adde a hundred more;
A thousand to that hundred; so kiss on,
To make that thousand up a million;
Treble that million, and when that is done
Let's kisse afresh, as when we first begun.

Robt. Herrick

They say

Here's to you both
a beautiful pair,
we celebrate
your love affair.

THIS HEART WITH A LITTLE ONE IN IT,
IS TO GIVE YOU TO UNDERSTAND,
THAT HEARTS CAN BE UNITED.
Nancy Luce

Nobody has ever measured, not even poets, how much the heart can hold. ♥ Zelda Fitzgerald

Thy loving smile will surely hail The love gift of a fairy tale.
♥ Lewis Carroll

It seems I should be homesick for you even in heaven. ♥ Louisa May Alcott

High heels were invented by a woman who'd been kissed on the forehead.
♥ Christopher Morley

The water is wide, I cannot cross o'er.
Neither have I the wings to fly.
Build me a boat that can carry two,
And both shall row, my Love and I.
♥ From an American Folk Song

To us

CAROLYN
MILLS
1904

You are always new to me;
The last of your kisses
was ever the sweetest.
♥ JOHN KEATS

If you would be loved,
love & be loveable.
♥ Benjamin Franklin

The modern rule is that
every woman must be her own
chaperone. ♥ Amy Vanderbilt

Tell me who admires you & loves you,
& I will tell you who you are.
♥ CHARLES AUGUSTIN SAINTE-BEAUVE

All I need to know about love I learned from the
song Hey Jude. ♥ James M. Stewart

Love is a fire. But whether it's going to warm
your hearth or burn down your house, you
never can tell. ♥ Joan Crawford

I love thee like pudding
If thou wert pie, I'd eat thee.
♥ John Ray

So much as she loves his love of her; Then

loves she her lover For love of her

loves, Or love of her love of her lover?

...You take a lover who looks at you like maybe you are magic.
❤ Frida Kahlo

I want to do with you what spring does with the cherry trees.
Pablo Neruda

Let's get loose with compassion — Let's drown in the delicious ambience of LOVE.
Hafez

There is wisdom of the head, and there is wisdom of the heart.
❤ Charles Dickens

WHAT COMES FROM THE HEART GOES TO THE HEART.
❤ Samuel Taylor Coleridge

He gave her a look you could pour on a waffle.
Ring Lardner

The wind is rushing after us, & the clouds are flying after us, and the moon is plunging after us, & the whole wild night is in pursuit of us.
❤ CHARLES DICKENS

Sensuality, wanting a religion, invented love.
❤ Natalie Clifford Barney

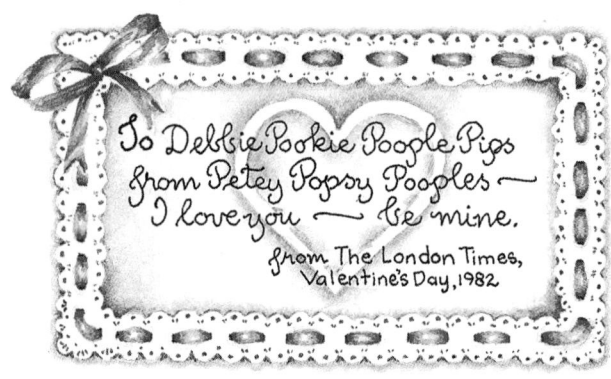

To Debbie Pookie Poople Pigs
from Petey Popsy Pooples —
I love you — be mine.

from The London Times,
Valentine's Day, 1982

THE GREEK BIOGRAPHER
PLUTARCH WROTE THAT
THE BODY OF ALEXANDER
THE GREAT GAVE OFF
THE SCENT OF VIOLETS.

Yum...

TWO SOULS BUT
WITH A SINGLE
THOUGHT—
TWO HEARTS
THAT BEAT
AS ONE.
Maria Lovell

Strephon kissed me in the spring,
Robin in the fall,
But Colin only looked at me
And never kissed at all.
Strephon's kiss was lost in jest,
Robin's lost in play,
But the kiss in Colin's eyes
Haunts me night and day.

♥ Sara Teasdale

Across the gateway of my heart
I wrote 'No Thoroughfare,'
But love came laughing by,
and cried: 'I enter everywhere.'
♥ Herbert Shipman

I wasn't kissing her, I was
whispering in her mouth.
♥ Chico Marx

I wish I were the China cup from which you
drink your tea,
then everytime you take a sip, I would mean
a kiss for me. ♥ FROM AN OLD VALENTINE

A soulmate is someone who has the locks that fit our keys, and keys to fit our locks. ♥ Richard Bach

Love is the one wild card.
♥ Taylor Swift

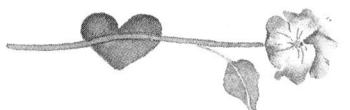

When this you see Remember me ♥

So lucky to be the one you run to see ♪
In the evening when the day is through...
TIME AFTER TIME
♥ Sammy Cahn

Once in a while, right in the middle of an ordinary life, love gives us a fairy tale.
♥ Anon.

The herdsman & the fairy were married with two gold rings at the parish church. He stayed a herdsman. His fairy wife never gave him the slightest trouble.
♥ FRENCH FOLKTALES

...We've only just begun to live... white lace & promises, a kiss for luck & we're on our way...
The Carpenters

They slipped briskly into an intimacy from which they never recovered. ♥ F. Scott Fitzgerald

Love isn't something you find ~ love is something that finds you. ♥ Loretta Young

For where thy treasure is, there also will thy heart be. ♥ Matthew 6:21

FORTUNE & LOVE FAVOR THE BRAVE. ♥ Ovid

A happy marriage is a long conversation which always seems too short. ♥ Andre Maurois

Moons and tunes and ferris wheels, the dizzy dancing way you feel, as every fairy tale comes true... ♥ Joni Mitchell

And they lived happily ever after. ♥ ANON.

Love

A JOY SHARED IS A JOY DOUBLED

Don't hurry, take your time, be sure, it's never too late for love. ♥ Susan Branch

You're all dressed up to go dreaming
Now don't tell me I'm wrong
And what a night to go dreaming
Mind if I tag along?

MOONLIGHT BECOMES YOU

Heaven will be no heaven to me
if I do not meet my wife there.
♥ Andrew Jackson

When he is wounded, I bleed. ♥ Abigail Adams

I DO, I DO, I DO, I DO, I DO.

And suddenly I realised
that it would all happen,
I would be his wife, we would walk
in the garden together, we would
stroll down that path in the valley
to the shingle beach. I knew how
I would stand on the steps after
breakfast, looking at the day,
throwing crumbs to the birds,
and later wander out in a
shady hat with long scissors
in my hand, and cut flowers
for the house. ♥

Daphne du Maurier

WHEN TWO PEOPLE
LOVE EACH OTHER,
THEY DON'T LOOK
AT EACH OTHER,
THEY LOOK IN
THE SAME
DIRECTION.

Ginger Rogers

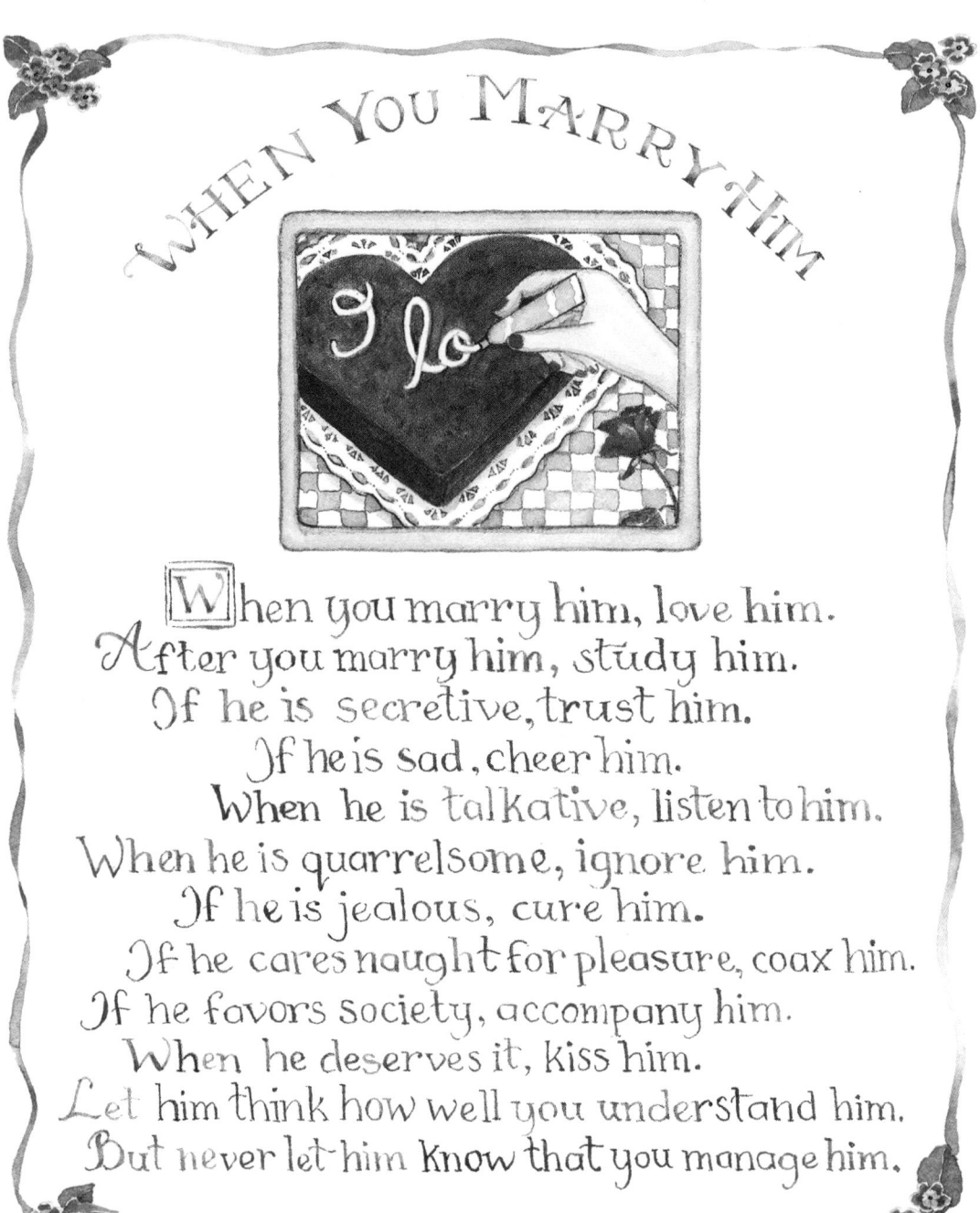

WHEN YOU MARRY HIM

When you marry him, love him.
After you marry him, study him.
If he is secretive, trust him.
If he is sad, cheer him.
When he is talkative, listen to him.
When he is quarrelsome, ignore him.
If he is jealous, cure him.
If he cares naught for pleasure, coax him.
If he favors society, accompany him.
When he deserves it, kiss him.
Let him think how well you understand him.
But never let him know that you manage him.

Pair found framed in an antique store. ♥ Unattributed old prints ♥ SB

WHEN YOU MARRY HER

When you marry her, love her.
After you marry her, study her.
When she is blue, cheer her.
When she is talkative,
        by all means listen to her.
If she dresses well, compliment her.
When she is cross, humor her.
When she does you a favor, kiss her.
If she is jealous, cure her.
If she is lonely, comfort her.
When she looks pretty, tell her so.
Let her feel how well you understand her.
But never let her know she isn't boss.

I HAVE LEARNED THAT ONLY TWO THINGS ARE NECESSARY TO KEEP ONE'S WIFE HAPPY. FIRST, LET HER THINK SHE IS HAVING HER OWN WAY. AND SECOND, LET HER HAVE IT.
♥ LYNDON JOHNSON

TE ADORO MY LITTLE PETTY PET

Oh Finger with the circlet slight
That keeps it warm and cosy
Wee winsome third left-handed doight
So white and warm and rosy
More taper digits there may be
More lips may kiss and cling on
This tiny finger's best to me
The one I put the ring on.

H. Cholmondeley-Pennell

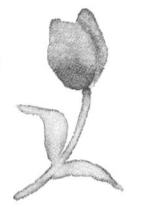

Little Red Riding Hood was my first love. I felt that if I could have married Little Red Riding Hood, I should have known happiness.
♥ CHARLES DICKENS

EVERYBODY LOVES A BABY THAT'S WHY I'M IN LOVE WITH YOU. ♥ Gus Kahn

Grow up, fall in love, get a little house, plant some roses, get a kitty, live happily ever after. What could be more simple? Every movie had it in it. ♥ JB

BLESSINGS LOVE

I don't want sunbursts or marble halls. I just want you. L.M. Montgomery ♥

Some fall in love with women who are rich, aristocratic or stupid. I am attracted by those who mysteriously hold out a promise of the integrity which I have lost; unsubdued daughters of Isis, beautiful as night, tumultuous as the moon-stirred Atlantic. ♥ Cyril Connolly

Grow old along with me
the best is yet to be . . .
♥ Robt. Browning

Wild Thing . . .
You make my
Heart Sing♪
♥ The Troggs

Give me my Romeo; and when
he shall die,
Take him and cut him out in little
stars,
And he will make the face of
heaven so fine
That all the world will be in
love with night
And pay no worship to the
garish sun.

♥ William Shakespeare

LOVE
is love's reward.
♥ John Dryden

The kiss originated when the first male
reptile licked the first female reptile,
implying in a subtle, complimentary way
that she was as succulent as the small
reptile he had for dinner the night before.

♥ F. Scott Fitzgerald

True love means planning a life for two,
Being together the whole day through...
True love means waiting & hoping that soon
Wishes we've made will come true...
♥ RAY HILDEBRAND... Hey Paula

Above all else,
    guard your heart.
        Proverbs 4:23

I love you

If you cry, catch your tears in a cup,
    sprinkle them on your lover's
pillow ~ he will experience a great change of heart.
        ♥ Susan Branch

THEY AREN'T LONG, THE DAYS OF WINE AND ROSES! ♥ E. DOWSON

A person can be lonely even if he
    is loved by many people, because
he's still not the "One and Only"
    to anyone. ♥ANNE FRANK

Tonight.
Same time.
Same place.
    SB

The heart speaks ♥ in many ways.
        Jean Racine

Love in its essence is spiritual fire.
        ♥ Emanuel Swedenborg

Go to your bosom; knock there, & ask your heart what it doth know. ♥ William Shakespeare

You should be kissed, & often, by someone who knows how. ♥ Rhett Butler (Margaret Mitchell)

Give a man a fish & he eats for a day. Teach him how to fish & you get rid of him for the whole weekend. ♥ Zenna Schaffer

And all the time we must be apart, I keep a candle in my heart. ♥ Mary E. Linton

She said she usually cried at least once a day not because she was sad but because the world was so beautiful & life was so short. ♥ BRIAN ANDREAS

Outside our kitchen window, I watch him feed her. ♥ (my kind of guy.)

Susan Branch

I LOVE YOU. YOU'RE PERFECT. (NOW CHANGE.) ♥ Anonymous

It's better to have a heart without words, than to have words without a heart. ♥ *Mahatma Gandhi*

Like the grasses
showing tender faces
to each other,
thus should we do,
for this is
the wish of the
Grandfathers
of the
World.

Black Elk

Some people assert that this was not the work of fairy enchantment, but that love alone brought about the transformation. ♥ FRENCH FOLKTALES

The way to avoid divorce is that no one leaves.
♥ Susan Branch

I have no notion of loving people by halves, it is not in my nature. ♥ Jane Austen

And still, after all this time, the Sun has never said to the Earth, "You owe me." Look what happens with love like that. It lights up the sky.
♥ H a f e z

Lovely love loves to love love.
♥ after James Joyce

Happy Wife, Happy Life.
♥ proverb

While her lips talked culture, her heart was planning to invite him to tea. ♥
E. M. Forster

TEA?

Was there anything more romantic than squashing together into a phone booth and closing the folding doors? The wool of his jacket on your cheek, the jingling of dimes as they go into the slot, the long distance operator, the expectation, the wait with kisses, the excitement of the connection, the sharing of the receiver. All made even better if it was raining.
♥ Susan Branch

212

It's all life is **J**ust going around kissing people.
F. Scott Fitzgerald

If nature has made you a giver, your hands are born open, and so is your heart.
♥ FRANCES HODGSON BURNETT

Don't never go looking for love girl. Just wait. It'll come. ♥ Sonia Sanchez

Wendy, Wendy, when you are sleeping in your silly bed you might be flying about with me saying funny things to the stars.
J. M. Barrie ♥ Peter Pan

i think it bespeaks a generous nature, a man who can cook. ♥ JILLY COOPER

♫...**W**ell, I walked to my house like a good girl should, he followed me to my house like I knew he would... ♪
♥ Doris Day

With two bright eyes, my star, my love, Thou lookest on the stars above; Ah, would that I the heaven might be, With a million eyes to look upon thee.
♥ Plato

OWN YOURSELF

THINK IT OVER

BE SURE

TAKE YOUR TIME

LOOK BEFORE YOU LEAP

TO THINE OWNSELF BE TRUE

FOREVER IS A LONG, LONG TIME...

STAY IN THE TREE

ADVICE TO WOMEN

SELF-LOVE COMES FIRST ♥

"The art of flirtation is dying. A man & woman are either in love these days or just friends. In the realm of love, reticence & sophistication go hand in hand, for one of the joys of life is discovery." ♥ Marya Mannes

...he placed his hands on my mind before he reached for my waist...
♥ Rupi Kaur

WITH LOVE

If you love someone, set them free. If they come back, they're yours, if they don't, they never were. ♥ *Richard Bach*

LOVE

I haven't had that one great love, which is good. I don't want that to be in the past, I want it to be in the future.

♥ *Taylor Swift*

BREAKING UP · LOST INNOCENCE · BROKEN HEARTS

The cure for anything
is salt~

Sweat, tears, or
the sea.
♥ Isak Dinesen

I wish I had no heart, it aches so.
♥ Louisa May Alcott

Dark Clouds

Then the blue shadows will
fall all over town...
Ronnie Milsap

Her mind was all disorder. The past, present, future,
everything was terrible. 💔 *Jane Austen*

LOVE STINKS
💙 Peter Wolf and Seth Justman

Love hurts, love scars, love wounds, love mars...
💔 *The Everly Brothers*

♪ WHAT'S LOVE GOT TO DO, GOT TO DO WITH IT... ♪
💙 TERRY BRITTEN & GRAHAM LYLE

When the dance was over she curtsied, & when the
King looked 'round again she had vanished &
none knew whither. ♥ *Brothers Grimm*

Life must go on; I forget just why.
♥ *Edna St. Vincent Millay*

My life is a perfect
graveyard of
buried hopes.
L. M. Montgomery

And the devil said to
Simon Legree,
"I like your style,
so wicked & free."
♥ *Vachel Lindsay*

♪ Although I can't dismiss the memory of his kiss... ♪ I guess he's not for me... *Ira Gershwin*

Grief is the price we pay for love. *Queen Elizabeth II*

The ocean is filled with tears, & the sea turns into a mirror... ♥ Tom Waits

Nothing happens to any man that he is not formed by nature to bear. ♥ MARCUS AURELIUS

Sometimes I wonder if men & women really suit each other. Perhaps they should live next door & just visit now & then. ♥ *Katharine Hepburn*

Silence isn't always golden, you know. Sometimes it's just plain yellow. ♥ *Jan Kemp*

Love is or it ain't. Thin love ain't love at all. ♥ *Toni Morrison*

It was no one's fault but my own. I'd married without a contingency plan. ♥ *Susan Branch*

That's when I realized that in order for me to survive this breakup one of us had to leave the pond, and since it obviously wasn't going to be the big happy fish, it would have to be me. ♥ *Susan Branch*

Although the world is full of suffering it is also full of the overcoming of it. ♥ Helen Keller

No Day is so bad it can't be fixed with a nap. ♥ Carrie Snow

The moving finger writes & having written, moves on. All thy piety nor all thy wit can cancel half a line of it. ♥ Omar Khayyam

If only the brother had his human form, it would have been a wonderful life. ♥ Brothers Grimm

Anxiety is the dizziness of freedom. ♥ Kierkegaard

If you're going through hell, keep going. ♥ Winston Churchill

Don't cry because it's over, smile because he's finally someone else's problem. ♥ Anonymous

We must be willing to let go of the life we planned so as to have the life that is waiting for us. ♥ Joseph Campbell

Smile in the mirror. Do it every morning & soon you'll start seeing a big difference in your life. ♥ Yoko Ono

Never allow someone to be your priority while allowing yourself to be their option. ♥ Mark Twain

TALK TO THE HAND

I love my liberty too well to be in a hurry to give it up for any mortal man. ♥ Louisa May Alcott

HOP ON THE BUS, GUS
Thank You Paul Simon

Hate to see you eat & run but here's your hat & donut. ♥ Lorrie Dominguez

Crowd cheers as jury clears redhead of driving car over refrigerator repairman. Roxie Hart, newspaper headline

If you've never eaten while crying you don't know what life tastes like. ♥ Johann Wolfgang von Goethe

Take me or leave me; or, as is the usual order of things, both. ♥ Dorothy Parker

DEAD as a DOORNAIL.
— Wm. Shakespeare

... all that she had had, and all that she missed, were lost together, and were twice lost in this landslide of remembered losses. ♥ Katherine Anne Porter

Expectation is the root of all heartache. ♥ Wm. Shakespeare

Goodbye, yellow brick road . . .

WAH

TROUBLE IN RIVER CITY

Sometimes we're at our most courageous best when we just keep going. ♥ Susan Branch

♫ Everytime we say goodbye I die a little . . . ♪
♥ Cole Porter

There's something n a s t y in the wood shed.
Stella Gibbons COLD COMFORT FARM

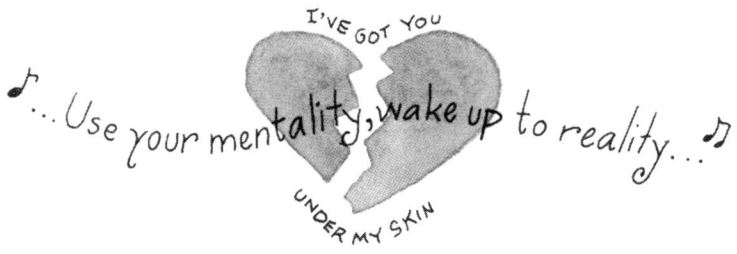

I'VE GOT YOU

♪ . . . Use your mentality, wake up to reality . . . ♫

UNDER MY SKIN

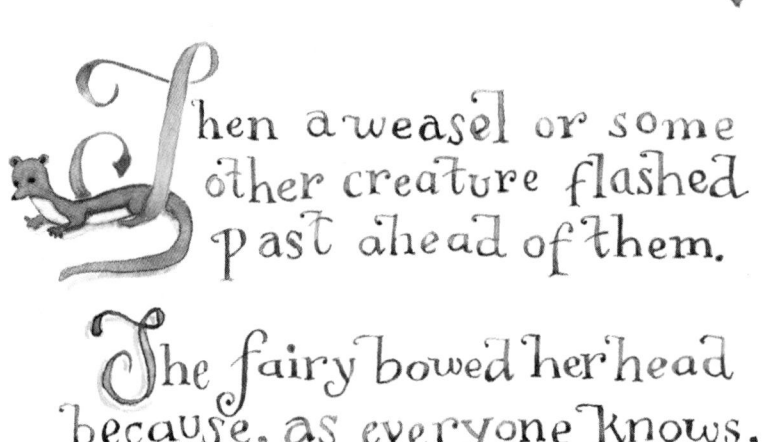

Then a weasel or some other creature flashed past ahead of them.

The fairy bowed her head because, as everyone knows, that's not a good sign.
♥ French Fairy Tales

Well, you can tell by the way I use my walk I'm a woman's man: no time to talk... ♪
♥ The Bee Gees

MEN, SCHMEN.

When in doubt, don't.
♥ Benjamin Franklin

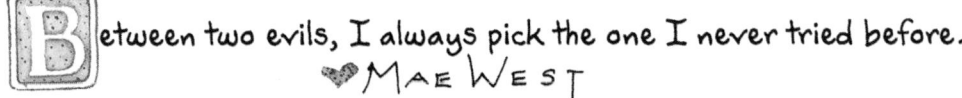

Between two evils, I always pick the one I never tried before.
♥ MAE WEST

The main difference between men & women is that men are maniacs & women are idiots. ♥ Rebecca West

Some mistakes are too much fun to make only once.
♥ Margaret Mitchell

When you see crazy coming, cross the street. ♥ Diana Bowlby

Psychotics, say what you want about them, tend to make the first move. ♥ DAVID FOSTER WALLACE

Every night I turn my fears over to God. He's going to be up all night anyway. ♥ Anon.

The true way to soften one's troubles is to solace those of others. ♥ Mme. de Maintenon

You CAN BURY A LOT of TROUBLES DIGGING IN THE DIRT.

Experience is a brutal teacher, but you do learn. ♥ C.S. Lewis

I put on my list all the busy, useful independent spinsters I know, for liberty is a better husband than love to many of us. ♥ Louisa May Alcott

And when the world seems to be falling apart around you, create something, put a flower in a vase, bake a pie, draw a picture, knit socks. ♥ Susan Branch

The way I see it, if you want the rainbow, you gotta put up with the rain. ♥ Dolly Parton

We have it in our power to begin the world over again. ♥ Thomas Paine

I remember the way we parted,
the day and the way we met;
You hoped we were both brokenhearted
and knew we should both forget.
And the best and the worst of this is
that neither is most to blame,
If you have forgotten my kisses and
I have forgotten your name.

♥ A.C. Swinburne ♥

The wound is the place
where the light enters you.
♥ Rumi 1260

You can't truly have an
open heart until it's
been broken.
Alice Walker

Sadness is
but a wall
between
two gardens
♥ Kahlil Gibran

Walk on air
against
your better judgement.
♥ Seamus Heaney

Too bad, so sad. ♥

The broken heart. You think you will die, but you just keep living, day after terrible day. ♥ Charles Dickens

Every sorrow suggests a thousand songs, & every song recalls a thousand sorrows, & so they are infinite in number, & all the same.
♥ MARILYNNE ROBINSON

COMFORT ME WITH APPLES FOR I AM SICK OF LOVE.
Song of Solomon 2:5

HYACINTHS *for the* SOUL

If, of thy mortal goods   thou art bereft,
& from thy slender   store two loaves
alone to thee   are left,
Sell one & from   the dole,
Buy hyacinths to   feed thy soul.

Sa'di, The Gulistan, 1258

The trouble is not that I am single & likely to stay single, but that I am lonely & likely to stay lonely.
Charlotte Brontë

IT COULD HAVE TURNED OUT DIFFERENTLY, I SUPPOSE.

BUT IT DIDN'T.

Mansfield Park

Loneliness and the feeling of being unwanted is the most terrible poverty.
♥ Mother Teresa

227

Submission to what people call their 'lot' is simply ignoble. If your lot makes you cry and be wretched, get rid of it and take another. ♥ Elizabeth von Arnim

HELP ONE ANOTHER IS PART OF THE RELIGION OF OUR SISTERHOOD. Louisa May Alcott

GIRLTALK

Grief is love with nowhere to go. ♥ Jamie Anderson

THE BEST WAY TO MEND A BROKEN HEART IS TIME & GIRLFRIENDS. ♥ GWYNETH PALTROW

Wait. In a little while, everything will change. ♥ Susan Branch

Tea for One

TRY A DESSERT-TEA LIKE LAVENDER EARL GREY... HAVE IT WITH HONEY & CREAM; A SOFT EGG SALAD SANDWICH WITHOUT CRUST, A COOKIE & a good book.

LOVE THE ONE YOU'RE WITH

SB

You gotta kiss a lot of Frogs before you find Prince Charming. ♥ ANON.

KISS?

"Wendy," Peter Pan continued in a voice no woman has ever yet been able to resist, "Wendy, one girl is more use than 20 boys." ♥ J.M. Barrie

The past is a foreign country. They do things differently there. ♥ L. P. Hartley

IF HE HAS BEEN UNFAITHFUL—TO GAIN YOU
BACK HE MUST GATHER HAIR FROM THE FACE
OF A WOLF (INCLUDING WHISKERS) – THEN BURN
THEM + DRINK THE ASHES IN A SHOTGLASS FULL
OF SOUR MILK. IF HE LIVES, YOU MAY FORGIVE HIM + BE
CONFIDENT OF HIS FIDELITY. ♥ (P.S. He must not harm the wolf.)
♥ Susan Branch

IT TAKES A PRETTY SPECIAL MAN TO TAKE
THE PLACE OF NO MAN AT ALL. ♥ Susan Branch

Delicious tears! the heart's own dew. ♥ L. E. Landon

Captain Hook: Look who's still a fairy.   ⸙ poor baby ⸙
Tinkerbelle: Look who's still a pirate.
                    J. M. Barrie

CUE THE MUSIC
Glory days, well they'll
        pass you by
Glory days, in the wink of a young girl's eye...
                    ♫ BRUCE SPRINGSTEEN

Hell is empty and all the devils are here. ♥ Wm. Shakespeare

♪ **And** DON'T TELL ME WHAT TO DO... ♫
                    ♥ HELEN REDDY

My soul is crushed, my spirit sore;
        I do not like me anymore.
I cavil, quarrel, grumble, grouse.
I ponder on the narrow house.
I shudder at the thought of men...
I'm due to fall in love again.
        ♥ Dorothy Parker

TIME HEALS

229

...And in her eyes you see nothing, no sign of love behind the tears, cried for no one, a love that should have lasted years...
♥ The Beatles

♪ She makes love just like a woman But she breaks just like a little girl... ♥ Bob Dylan

"I have lost my dew drop," cried the flower to the morning sky that lost all its stars.
♥ Rabindranath Tagore

EAT A BULLFROG FIRST THING IN THE MORNING... & NOTHING WORSE CAN HAPPEN TO YOU THE REST OF THE DAY.
♥ Mark Twain

No one ever told me that grief felt so much like fear. ♥ C. S. Lewis

PEOPLE LIVE THROUGH SUCH PAIN ONLY ONCE. PAIN COMES AGAIN, BUT IT finds A TOUGHER SURFACE. Willa Cather

I would wake up at night, longing for something that no longer existed, much more than just him, or the marriage, or even my old life, I mourned for the believing thing. ♥ Susan Branch

The fairies looked at him & all shook their heads at once.
The Brown Fairy Book

FINDING THE GOOD IN GOODBYE

"AFTER A YEAR IN THERAPY, MY PSYCHIATRIST SAID TO ME, "MAYBE LIFE ISN'T for EVERYONE." *Larry Brown*

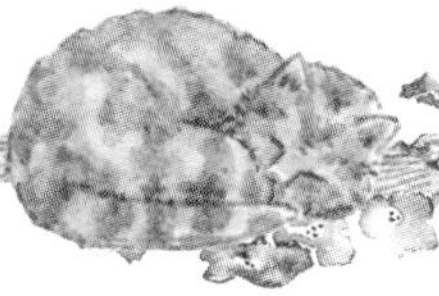

TRIED & TRUE

Recipe for
STARTING OVER

HOMEMADE & FROM SCRATCH

4 c. silence
SEASONED WITH
1 lb. bird song
3 pr. flannel jammies
2 gal. telephone, room temp.
75 bottles of wine (to drink with,)
700 lbs. girlfriends
1-5 kitties (or, to taste)

MIX WELL. LET SIT SIX YEARS.

Susan Branch

I've locked my heart, I'll keep my feelings there,
I've stocked my heart with icy, frigid air,
And I mean to care for no one,
because I'm through with love.
♥ Marilyn Monroe

Change is not always a choice. How you deal with it is. ♥ Susan Branch

She made herself stronger by fighting with the wind. ♥ FRANCES HODGSON BURNETT

Nothing on earth can make up for the loss of one who has loved you. ♥ Selma Lagerlöf

Even on my weakest days I get a little bit stronger. ♥ SARA EVANS

I can't think of any sorrow in the world that a hot bath wouldn't help, just a little bit. ♥ Susan Glaspell

INHALE THE FUTURE, Exhale the past. ♥ AUTHOR UNKNOWN

The secret of change is to focus all your energy, not on fighting the old, but on building the new. ♥ Socrates

...I'M NOT AFRAID OF STORMS FOR I'M LEARNING HOW TO SAIL MY SHIP. ♥ LOUISA MAY ALCOTT

No one is useless in this world who lightens the burden of it to anyone else. ♥ Charles Dickens

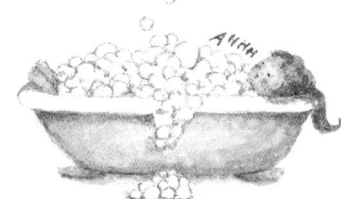

Breathe, darling. This is just a chapter, it's not the whole story. ♥ C.L. Lewis 🌸

Because, as they say in France, "It is overdoing the thing to die of love."

Swim out of your little pond. ♥ Rumi

A ship in harbor is safe, but that's not what ships are built for. ♥ John A. Shedd

It is easier to live through someone else than to become complete yourself. ♥ Betty Friedan

Stories were full of hearts being broken by love, but what really broke a heart was taking away its dream. ♥ Pearl S. Buck

Among the farewells, see you soon, I have no time, & stormy silences, I met someone...that someone, is me. ♥ Efrat Cybulkiewicz

Forgiving is not about forgetting, it's letting go of the hurt. ♥ Mary McLeod Bethune

Hang on to your hat, hold on to your hope, & wind the clock, for tomorrow is another day. ♥ E.B. White

I've been Miss Misery for the last time.
♥ Taylor Swift

If you can't live without me why aren't you dead yet?
♥ Cynthia Heimel

Now the maiden lived all alone in the cottage. She kept herself busy by spinning, weaving & sewing and bringing cow parsley from the meadow. Grimm's Fairy Tales

I didn't understand why I had to be the one to be forgiven, but I went ahead and forgave myself anyway. They all said I had to do it, and I knew it was the right thing, because for some reason, it made me cry. ♥ SUSAN BRANCH

What you seek is seeking you. ❧ RUMI

Crying does not indicate that you are weak. Since birth, it has always been a sign that you are alive.
♥ Charlotte Brontë

MINE ENEMY IS GRIEF...ONE OF US MUST DIE. ♥ PROCTER, 1858

So every morning I spit in his coffee. He doesn't know. I feel better; everyone's happy.
♥ Author unknown

Her Little Girl was Late Arriving Home from school so the Mother began to scold her, but stopped & asked, "Why are you so late?" "I had to help another girl. She was in trouble," replied the daughter. "What did you do to help her?" "Oh, I sat down & helped her cry."
♥ Author Unknown

"We're growing up and I don't like it," said Tacy.
♥ Maud Hart Lovelace

Don't ever think that a ravaged heart is all done with life, because miracles can happen.
♥ Susan Branch

I thought that spring must last for ever more — For I was young, and loved, and it was May.
♥ Vera Brittain

*O*ut beyond the world of ideas of wrong doing & right doing, there is a field. I will meet you there. ♥ RUMI

I wouldn't want to marry anybody who was wicked, but I think I'd like it if he could be wicked & wouldn't. ♥ L·M· Montgomery

SAY TO YOURSELF,

"NEXT?"

I stay cool & dig all jive, that's the way I stay alive. My motto, as I live & learn, is dig & be dug in return. ♥ Langston Hughes

*V*ARIETY IS THE SPICE OF LIFE. ♥ William Cowper

It's Raining Men
Hallelujah?

*F*orgive someone. Have your own personal Amnesty Day. ♥ Susan Branch

*H*olding on to anger is like drinking poison and expecting the other person to die. ♥ Gautama Buddha

IT'S ASTONISHING HOW SHORT A TIME IT TAKES FOR VERY WONDERFUL THINGS TO HAPPEN. ♥ *Frances Burnette*

AFTER ALL, MY ERSTWHILE DEAR, MY NO LONGER CHERISHED, NEED WE SAY IT WAS NOT LOVE, JUST BECAUSE IT PERISHED?
♥ *Edna St. Vincent Millay*

Though lovers be lost, not so love. ♥ *Dylan Thomas*

I love. I have loved. I will love.
♥ *I Capture the Castle*

It's relaxing to go out with my ex-wife because she already knows I'm an idiot. ♥ *Warren Thomas*

The universal sorrow hits me about once a week. Bang! I'm, oh well. 😫 And then I get back to it.
♥ *John Lennon*

All shall be well, all shall be well, all manner of things shall be well.
Julian of Norwich

THE ONLY FEELING STRONGER THAN LOSS IS LOVE. ♥
♥ *Susan Branch*

Sometimes good things fall apart so better things can fall together.
♥ *Marilyn Monroe*

We shall draw from the heart of suffering itself, the means of inspiration & survival. ♥ *Winston Churchill*

LET US PUT OUR MINDS TOGETHER AND SEE WHAT KIND OF LIFE WE CAN MAKE FOR OUR CHILDREN.

Sitting Bull

Red and Yellow, Black and White,
   They are precious in his sight,
   Jesus loves   the little children
   of the world.   ♥ *George F. Root*

No one has yet realized the wealth of sympathy, the kindness & generosity hidden in the soul of a child. ♥ *Emma Goldman*

THE AMERICAN DREAM

God shed His grace on thee. ♥ K. Bates

If seeds in the black earth can turn into such beautiful roses, what might the heart of man become in its long journey toward the stars?
♥ G.K. Chesterton

What we do matters. ♥

IF NOT US, THEN Who? IF NOT NOW, THEN When?

Life is politics; you do it, or it does you.
♥ Bangamniki Habyarimana

An eye for an eye only ends up making the whole world blind.
♥ Gandhi

Truth will ultimately prevail where there are pains to bring it to light.
♥ George Washington

I miss those days when there was only one idiot per village. Anon.

Sometimes I wonder whether the world is being run by smart people who are putting us on Or by imbeciles who really mean it. ♥ Mark Twain

Don't find fault, find a remedy; anybody can complain.
♥ Henry Ford

There are far too many men in politics.
♥ Hermione Gingold

What we now call "politically correct," my mom called "manners." ♥ Susan Branch

A free press, can, of course, be good or bad, but, most certainly without freedom, the press will never be anything but bad.
♥ Albert Camus

The only security of all is in a free press. ♥ Thomas Jefferson

Pit race against race, religion against religion, prejudice against prejudice. Divide and conquer! We must not let that happen here.
♥ Eleanor Roosevelt

Living is easy with eyes closed...
♥ John Lennon

What luck for rulers that men do not think.
ADOLF HITLER

When someone shows you who they are, believe them.
♥ Maya Angelou

When I do good, I feel good. When I do bad, I feel bad. And that's my religion.
♥ Abraham Lincoln

When you make a choice, you change the future.
♥ Deepak Chopra

We can easily forgive a child who is afraid of the dark; the real tragedy of life is when men are afraid of the light. ♥ P L A T O

It's not the things we don't know that get us into trouble; it's the things we do know that ain't so. ♥ Will Rogers

It is impossible for a man to learn what he thinks he already knows. ♥ Epictetus

For though we love both the truth & our friends, piety requires us to honor the truth first. ♥ A R I S T O T L E

There are some people that if they don't know, you can't tell them. ♥ Louis Armstrong

IF STUPIDITY GOT US INTO THIS MESS, THEN WHY CAN'T IT GET US OUT? ♥ Will Rogers

The object of life is not to be on the side of the majority but to escape finding oneself in the ranks of the insane. ♥ Marcus Aurelius

I LIKE TO SEE A MAN PROUD OF THE PLACE IN WHICH HE LIVES. I LIKE TO SEE A MAN LIVE SO HIS PLACE WILL BE PROUD OF HIM. ♥ Abraham Lincoln

A lie gets halfway around the world before the truth has a chance to get its pants on. ♥ Winston Churchill

We must do everything in our power to cease the behavior that makes children everywhere feel afraid. ♥ Alice Walker

As a woman I have no country. As a woman I want no country. As a woman, my country is the whole world. ♥ Virginia Woolf

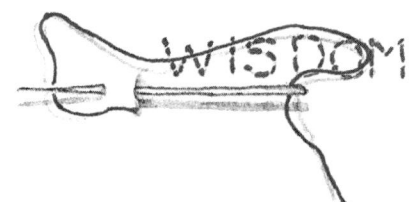

Always remember, you have within you the strength, the patience, & the passion to reach for the stars, to change the world. ♥ Harriet Tubman

I am sure if the mothers of various nations could meet, there would be no more wars. ♥ E.M. Forster

Give me your tired, your poor, your huddled masses yearning to breathe free.
FROM THE Emma Lazarus SONNET on the STATUE of LIBERTY

Every politician should have been born an orphan and remain a bachelor.
♥ LADY BIRD JOHNSON

Human Rights ARE Women's Rights AND Women's Rights are Human Rights ♥
Hillary Rodham Clinton

Common sense is seeing things as they are, & doing things as they ought to be. ♥ Harriet Beecher Stowe

A feminist is anyone who recognizes the equality & full humanity of all women & men. ♥ Gloria Steinem

FEMINISM HAS MORPHED INTO HUMANISM. STANDING ON TWO FEET OR FOUR; IF YOU HAVE A HEARTBEAT, YOU MATTER. ♥ SB

Remember, all men would be tyrants if they could. ♥ Abigail Adams

When will our consciences grow so tender that we will act to prevent human misery rather than avenge it? ♥ Eleanor Roosevelt

Religion without humanity is very poor human stuff. ♥ SOJOURNER TRUTH

Concentrated unaccountable economic power threatens the common good. ♥ Cynthia Moe-Lobeda

How wonderful it is that nobody need wait a single moment before starting to improve the world. ♥ ♥ ♥ Anne Frank

It is not female egotism to say that the future of mankind may very well be ours to determine. It is a fact. ♥ Shirley Chisholm

245

The American Dream

Nowadays it seems impossible That anyone could raise eight children on a one-person salary, but my parents didn't do it alone. After the war, our government & all Americans set themselves to rebuilding the country. College educations for returning soldiers & loans for new homes like ours were subsidized by the GI Bill. The government built new schools, like the ones we went to, as fast as they could; unions were strong; workers were protected. Everyone paid taxes, but corporations contributed 50% of their profit & the highest wage earners paid 70%. In order to make the whole country strong, most of the very rich managed to struggle through life with a mere 10 million in the bank. They were patriots & did not abandon us to take their money, their businesses, & their jobs away to foreign lands. There was dignity in the middle class; we had houses & jobs. Homelessness was rare. A parent could afford to stay home & take care of the kids, & everyone could go to Disneyland. It was really nice. The lovely American Dream.
♥ SB

Supporting women in politics (whose ideas you agree with of course) is also a way to make a change, because, as Jeannette Rankin said, "We're half the people, we should be half the congress." ♥ SB

Beautiful faces are those that wear Whole-souled honesty printed there.
♥ Ellen Palmer Allerton

Let every action aim solely at the common good. ♥ MARCUS AURELIUS

Everybody gets so much information all day long that they lose their common sense. ♥ Gertrude Stein

Common sense is not so common. ♥ Voltaire

A person who has planted a garden feels he has done something for the world. He belongs to the producers.
Charles Dudley Warner

Hurt not the EARTH, Neither the sea...
REVELATION 7:3

I am in favor of animal rights as well as human rights. That is the way of a whole human being.
♥ ♥ Abraham Lincoln ♥

THE FROG DOES NOT DRINK UP THE POND IN WHICH HE LIVES. ♥ NATIVE AMERICAN PROVERB

The assumption that animals are without rights and the illusion that our treatment of them has no moral significance is a positively outrageous example of Western crudity and barbarity. Universal compassion is the only guarantee of morality.
♥ Arthur Schopenhauer

Mockingbirds don't do one thing but make music for us to enjoy They don't eat up people's gardens, don't nest in corncribs, they don't do one thing but sing their hearts out for us. That's why it's a sin to kill a mockingbird. ♥ *Harper Lee*

HEAVEN IS UNDER OUR FEET AS WELL AS OVER OUR HEADS. ♥ *Henry David Thoreau*

What is the use of a house if you haven't got a tolerable planet to put it on? ♥ *Thoreau*

DO NOT LET SPACIOUS PLANS FOR A NEW WORLD DIVERT YOUR ENERGIES FROM SAVING WHAT IS LEFT OF THE OLD. ♥ *Winston Churchill*

IF YOU REALLY THINK THAT THE ENVIRONMENT IS LESS IMPORTANT THAN THE ECONOMY, TRY HOLDING YOUR BREATH WHILE YOU COUNT YOUR MONEY. ♥ *Guy McPherson*

TODAY IF YOU'RE NOT CONFUSED YOU'RE JUST NOT THINKING CLEARLY. ♥ *Irene Peter*

When you have an opportunity to talk to a member of Congress, I liken it to fishing, right? You know you have bait, you throw that bait out. KEITH McCOY, Sr. Director for Federal Relations Exxon Mobil

Did we aggressively fight against some of the climate science? Yes... Did we join some of these shadow groups to work against some of the early efforts? Yes, that's true. KEITH McCOY for EXXON

Earth provides enough to satisfy every man's need, but not every man's greed. ♥ *Mahatma Gandhi*

They're not listening now... perhaps they never will. ♥ DON McLEAN

We must accept finite disappointment, but never lose infinite hope. ♥ *Martin Luther King Jr.*

Conservation is Love is Patriotism. *SB*

The measure of intelligence is the ability to change. ♥ *Albert Einstein*

What is legal and for whom, depends on who is writing the laws.
♥ *SB*

The State of the Union

Courage, dear heart.
C. S. Lewis

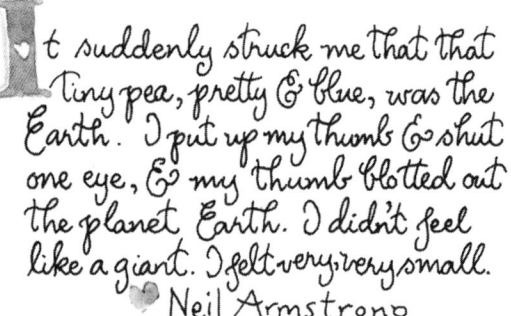

It suddenly struck me that that tiny pea, pretty & blue, was the Earth. I put up my thumb & shut one eye, & my thumb blotted out the planet Earth. I didn't feel like a giant. I felt very, very small.
♥ Neil Armstrong

Water and air, the two essential fluids on which all life depends, have become global garbage cans.
♥ *Jacques Costeau*

First & last, what is demanded of genius is love of truth.
♥ *Johann Wolfgang von Goethe*

Never wrestle with pigs. You both get dirty & the pig likes it.
George Bernard Shaw

MEN ARGUE.
NATURE ACTS.
♥ Voltaire

If I fall, I'll fall 5'4" forward in the fight for freedom.
♥ *Fannie Lou Hamer*

Common sense is instinct. Enough of it is genius.
♥ *George Bernard Shaw*

Really great men have a curious feeling that the greatness is not of them, but through them. And they see something divine in every other man and are endlessly, foolishly, incredibly, merciful. ♥ John Ruskin

Mankind was my business. The common welfare was my business; charity, mercy, compassion, & tolerance were all my business. ♥ Charles Dickens

A great man is always willing to be little. ♥ EMERSON

Thus out of small beginnings greater things have been produced by His hand that made all things of nothing, and gives being to all things that are; and, as one small candle may light a thousand, so the light here kindled hath shone on many . . . ♥ William Bradford

Kindness is in our power, even when fondness is not. ♥ Samuel Johnson

If we have no peace, it is because we have forgotten that we belong to each other. ♥ Mother Theresa

WE MUST LIVE TOGETHER AS BROTHERS OR PERISH TOGETHER AS FOOLS. ♥ Martin Luther King Jr.

I have decided to stick to love . . . Hate is too great a burden to bear. ♥ Martin Luther King Jr.

He drew a circle that shut me out ~
Heretic, rebel, a thing to flout.
But Love & I had the wit to win:
We drew a circle that took him in.
♥ Edwin Markham

To know even one life has breathed easier because you have lived, this is to have succeeded. ♥ RALPH WALDO EMERSON

History has remembered the kings & warriors because they destroyed; art has remembered the people because they created. ♥ Wm. Morris

USE YOUR POWERS for GOOD.

Do not act as if you were going to live ten thousand years. While you live, while it is in your power, be good.
♥ Marcus Aurelius

Pride is a necessary quality for a person — not vain or pompous pride, but basic honest pride in self, family, home, work & country. With it you will always stand tall. ♥ James A. Retzlaff

No one cares how much you know until they know how much you care.
♥ Theodore Roosevelt

Shouldn't all towns have a big old tree in the middle loaded with blossoms and buzzing with honeybees? There should be a law; it would give Congress something productive to do, and a way to use our tax money that I personally could endorse: trees.
♥ Susan Branch

BUT IN CAMELOT, CAMELOT! THOSE ARE THE LEGAL LAWS.

Why waste your money looking up your family tree? Just go into politics & your opponent will do it for you.
♥ Mark Twain

If everyone is thinking alike, then somebody isn't thinking.
♥ George Patton

I believe there's only one race, the human race.
♥ Rosa Parks

Frequently consider the connection of all things in the universe. We should not say, 'I am an Athenian' or 'I am a Roman' but, 'I am a citizen of the Universe.' ♥ Marcus Aurelius

A society grows great when old men plant trees whose shade they know they shall never sit in.
♥ GREEK PROVERB

Seems to me it ain't the world that's so bad but what we're doing to it, and all I'm saying is: see what a wonderful world it would be if only we'd give it a chance. Love, baby, love. That's the secret.
♥ Louis Armstrong

As long as you keep a person down, some part of you has to be down there to hold him down, so it means you cannot soar as you otherwise might. ♥ Marian Anderson

As you grow older, you'll see that white men cheat black men every day of your life, but let me tell you something and don't you forget it: whenever a white man does that to a black man, no matter who he is, how rich he is, or how fine a family he comes from, that white man is trash. ♥ Harper Lee

There's enough sorrow in the world, isn't there, without trying to invent it. ♥ E. M. Forster

If we ever closed the door to new Americans, our leadership in the world would soon be lost. ♥ Ronald Reagan

No one leaves home unless home is the mouth of a shark. ♥ Warsan Shire

Irving Berlin wrote GOD BLESS AMERICA as a THANK-YOU to the country that took him in.

Just remember, when someone has an accent, it means that he knows one more language than you. ♥ Sidney Sheldon

May God make our hearts so big the whole world falls in. ♥ Susan Branch

I swear to the Lord, I still can't see why Democracy means everyone but me. ♥ LANGSTON HUGHES

 If a political party does not have its foundation in the determination to advance a cause that is right and that is moral, then it is not a political party; it is merely a conspiracy to seize power. ♥ Dwight D. Eisenhower

When good people in any country cease their vigilance and struggle, then evil men prevail. ♥ Pearl S. Buck

 TEACH PEACE ♥ Colman McCarthy

ALL THAT IS ESSENTIAL FOR THE TRIUMPH OF EVIL IS THAT GOOD FOLKS DO NOTHING. ♥ EDMUND BURKE

Only crooks take the fifth. Donald Trump

Those who can make you believe absurdities can make you commit atrocities. ♥ Voltaire

ETERNAL VIGILANCE IS THE PRICE of LIBERTY. ☆ Thomas U.P. Charlton

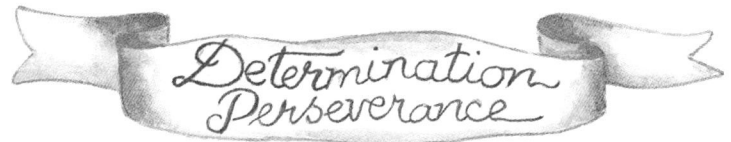 Determination Perseverance

What is done cannot be undone, but one can prevent it happening again. ♥ Anne Frank

Sometimes I feel like I'm on the wrong planet. I feel great when I'm inside the garden but the minute I go outside the gate I wonder, "What the hell am I doing here?" ♥ George Harrison

I don't want to live in the kind of world where we don't look out for each other. Not just the people that are close to us but anybody who needs a helping hand. I can't change the way anybody else thinks, or what they choose to do, but I can do my bit.
♡ Charles de Lint

"My country, right or wrong," is a thing no patriot would think of saying except in a desperate case. It's like saying, "My mother, drunk or sober."
♥ G. K. Chesterton

The only thing we have to fear, is fear itself.
♥ Franklin Roosevelt

Nothing is satisfactory that is one-sided.
♥ Charles Egbert Craddock

YOU NEVER REALLY UNDERSTAND A PERSON UNTIL YOU CONSIDER THINGS FROM HIS POINT OF VIEW. ♥ Harper Lee

He who does not oppose evil commands it to be done.
♥ Leonardo da Vinci

POVERTY IS THE Mother of CRIME ♥♥
Marcus Aurelius

Seeing their children touched and seared and wounded by race prejudice is one of the heaviest crosses which colored women have to bear. ♥ Mary Church Terrell

America the Beautiful
Imagine
♥ John Lennon

IT IS THE DUTY OF YOUTH TO BRING ITS FRESH NEW POWERS TO BEAR ON SOCIAL PROGRESS. EACH GENERATION OF YOUNG PEOPLE SHOULD BE TO THE WORLD LIKE A VAST RESERVE FORCE TO A TIRED ARMY. THEY SHOULD LIFT THE WORLD FORWARD. THAT IS WHAT THEY ARE FOR.
♥ Charlotte Perkins Gilman

Grownups do NOT get over being children. For good or for bad, all their secret beliefs about truth, goodness, & hope come from that place. ♥ Susan Branch

Yes, THE TRUTH MAY HURT, BUT LIES WILL CRIPPLE YOU.
♥ Stephen J. Scott

This boy is Ignorance. This girl is Want. Beware them both & all of their degree, but most of all, beware this boy.
♥ Charles Dickens

There is a way out of human suffering & any earnest person can find it. ♥ Vernon Howard

WE NEED A SEAT AT THE TABLE. IF WE'RE NOT AT THE TABLE, WE'RE PROBABLY ON THE MENU. ♥ Robert Mukaro Borrero

When we were little in the 1950s, Roy Rogers, Gene Autry, and the Lone Ranger showed us how heroic a good guy with a gun could be. Even the Mouseketeers wore guns. We wanted to be just like them. Our neighborhood swarmed with kids with cap guns and six-shooters ~ hiding behind apple crates, and falling down dead in the ivy beds. Now media is selling drones, as toys, to children. I'm very worried about the future of the sky. ♥ Susan Branch

A politician thinks of the next election. A statesman, of the next generation. ♥ JAMES FREEMAN CLARKE

EVERYTHING IS CONNECTED TO EVERYTHING ~ SB

An election is coming. Universal peace is declared, and the foxes have a sincere interest in prolonging the lives of the poultry. ♥ George Elliot

CYNICISM
KILL IT BEFORE IT MULTIPLIES

Alone we can do so little, Together we can do so much.
♥ HELEN KELLER

UNITED WE STAND

Hope, decency, & unity are not mere catchwords. ♥ Jon Ossof

What the people want is very simple — they want an America as good as its promise. ♥ Barbara Jordan

Politics ought to be the part-time profession of every citizen who would protect the rights and privileges of free people.
♥ Dwight D. Eisenhower

♪ WE ARE THE WORLD, WE ARE THE CHILDREN... ♫

Achievement has no color.
♥ *Abraham Lincoln*

Whatever you are, be a good one.
♥ *Abraham Lincoln*

NO COMPOSER HAS YET CAUGHT THIS RHYTHM OF AMERICA~ IT IS TOO MIGHTY FOR THE EARS OF MOST. ♥ ISADORA DUNCAN

Love your country with all your heart & soul and never stop trying to make it better.
♥ SUSAN BRANCH

The point of modern propaganda isn't only to misinform or push an agenda. It is to exhaust your critical thinking, to annihilate truth.
♥ *Garry Kasparov*

THE MOST VALUABLE POSSESSION YOU CAN OWN IS AN open heart. THE MOST POWERFUL WEAPON YOU CAN BE IS AN INSTRUMENT of PEACE.
♥ *Carlos Santana*

Compassion is the mother of moral courage.
SB

In the end, the American Dream is not a sprint, or even a marathon, but a relay. We pass the torch to our children.
♥ *Julian Castro*

The WAY To right wrongs is to turn the light of truth on them.
♥ *Ida B. Wells*

When I despair, I remember that all through history, the way of truth and love has always won. There have been tyrants and murderers, and for a time they can seem invincible, but in he end, they always fail. Think of it — always!
♥ *Mahatma Gandhi*

257

For too long politicians have told most of us that what's wrong with America is the rest of us. Them, them, them. But there is no them, there's only us. ♥ *Bill Clinton*

Wage peace. ♥ JUDITH HILL

IF YOU THINK EDUCATION IS EXPENSIVE, TRY IGNORANCE. ♥ *Jeff Rich*

Ignorance, in these days of Google and Fact-Check, is a choice. ♥ *SB*

ACTIVISM IS MY RENT for LIVING ON THE PLANET. ♥ *Alice Walker*

And so even though we face the difficulties of today & tomorrow, I still have a dream. It is a dream deeply rooted in the American Dream. ♥ *Martin Luther King Jr.*

Never doubt that a small group of thoughtful, committed citizens can change the world; indeed, it's the only thing that ever has. ♥ *Margaret Mead*

America will never be destroyed from the outside. If we falter & lose our freedoms, it will be because we destroyed ourselves. ♥ *Abraham Lincoln*

Go not in & out of court that thy name may not stink.
♥ *The Wisdom of Ani* (900 BC)

Don't part with your illusions. When they are gone, you may still exist, but you have ceased to live. ♥ Mark Twain

ELECTIONS BELONG TO THE PEOPLE. IT'S THEIR DECISION. IF THEY DECIDE TO TURN THEIR BACK ON THE FIRE & BURN THEIR BEHINDS, THEN THEY WILL JUST HAVE TO SIT ON THEIR BLISTERS. ♥ Abraham Lincoln

Historians know that most tyrannies have been possible because men moved too late. It is often essential to resist a tyranny before it exists. ♥ G.K. Chesterton

Never lose hope. Storms make people stronger & never last forever. ♥ Roy T. Bennett

When one with honeyed words but evil mind persuades the mob, great woes befall the state. ♥ Euripedes

The one thing you've got going: your one vote. ♥ Shirley Chisholm

You've got to vote for someone, it's a shame but it has to be done. ♥ Whoopi Goldberg

You can't solve all the world's problems. Now go wash your hands & come to the table. ♥ My mom

The American Dream

Don't throw the baby out with the bathwater. ♥ German proverb

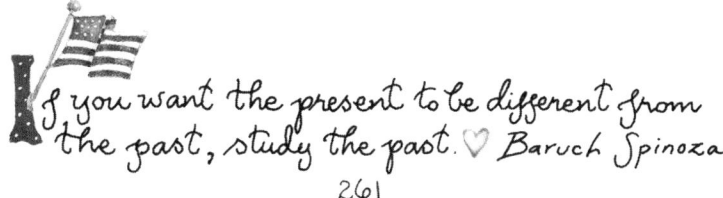

If you want the present to be different from the past, study the past. ♡ Baruch Spinoza

Faith is the bird that feels the light and sings when the dawn is still dark. . R. Tagore

COURAGE

Sky, be my depth; Wind, be my width & my height; World, my heart's span; Loneliness, Wings for my flight!
♥ Leonora Speyer

Pick yourself up, dust yourself off, & start all over again.
♥ Jerome Kern

Suddenly, the fairy stood before her. "Take heart," she said, "all will go now well."
♥ French Folktales

Light tomorrow with today.

Fear is the place dreams go to die.
♥ Susan Branch

It takes courage to grow up and become who you really are. ee cummings

Courage is the only Magick worth having. ♥ Erica Jong

Courage, dear heart. C. S. Lewis

Calm yourself. The world won't end today—
it's already tomorrow in Australia.
♥ Charles Schulz

Things that haven't been done before,
Those are the things to try;
Columbus dreamed of an unknown shore
At the rim of the far-flung sky.
♥ Edgar Guest

Security is a superstition. It does not exist in nature.
Life is either a daring adventure
or nothing at all.
♥ Helen Keller

FEAR

We can easily forgive a child who is
afraid of the dark; the real tragedy
of life is when men are afraid of the light.
♥ PLATO

The chief
ingredient
for success
is
Courage.
♥S.B.

Courage is doing what
you're afraid to do. There
is no courage unless you're
scared. ♥ EDDIE RICKENBACKER

Grab the broom of anger & drive off the beast of fear.
♥Zora Neale Hurston

If you look into your own heart & find nothing wrong there, what is there to worry about? What is there to fear?
♥ Confucius

Pray to God, but continue to row toward shore.
♥ Russian Proverb

Fear is a manipulative emotion that can trick us into living a boring life.
♥ Donald Miller

What difference do it make if the thing you scared of is real or not? ♥ Toni Morrison

I've been absolutely terrified every moment of my life and I've never let it keep me from doing a single thing I wanted to do. ♥ Georgia O'Keefe

So long as I know what's expected of me, I can manage.
♥ Frances Hodgson Burnett The Secret Garden

On Some hill of despair, the bonfire you kindle can light the great sky~ though it's true, of course, to make it burn you have to throw yourself in.
♥ Galway Kinnell

You've got to go out on a limb sometimes because that's where the fruit is.
♥ Will Rogers

I don't know where I'm going but I'm on my way. ♥ Voltaire

We are not interested in the possibilities of defeat. ♥ Queen Victoria

Look at how a single candle can both defy & define the darkness. ♥ Anne Frank

NEVER GIVE UP NO NO NEVER EVER

A SHIP IN HARBOR IS SAFE, BUT THAT'S NOT WHAT SHIPS ARE BUILT FOR. ♥ John A. Shedd

Let us be up and doing with a heart for any fate. Henry Wadsworth Longfellow

WHAT ISN'T TRIED WON'T WORK. ♥ Claude McDonald

Look for the helpers. Mr. Rogers ♥

ALL THE FLOWERS OF ALL THE TOMORROWS ARE IN THE SEEDS OF TODAY. ♥ Chinese proverb

266

"It's impossible," said pride.

"It's risky," said experience.

"It's pointless," said reason.

"Let's do it anyway," said the heart.
♡ Author Unknown

THE ONLY WAY TO IT IS THROUGH IT. ♥ Joan Fisher Dalz

The only people who never fail are those who never try.
♥ ILKA CHASE

The secret of getting ahead is getting started.
♥ Mark Twain

Turn and face the strange...
CH-CH-CH CHANGES...♪

I must try to make a fresh beginning. ♥ BEATRIX POTTER

Ring the bells that still can ring.
Forget your perfect offering.
There is a crack, a crack in everything
That's how the light gets in.
♥ LEONARD COHEN

FOR TO HAVE FAITH IS 💗 TO HAVE WINGS.
♥ J.M. Barrie

I know God will not give me anything I can't handle.
I just wish He didn't trust me so much. ♥ Mother Theresa

267

Never let the future disturb you. You will meet it, if you have to, with the same weapons of reason which today arm you against the present. ♥ Marcus Aurelius

CLIMB EVERY MOUNTAIN

It takes a lot of courage to show your dreams to someone else. ♥ Erma Bombeck

IT'S HARD TO BE BRAVE WHEN YOU'RE ONLY A VERY SMALL ANIMAL. A. A. Milne ♥

Life shrinks or expands in proportion to one's courage. ♥ Anais Nin

You can be afraid & still do it anyway. ♥ S.B.

There is a stubbornness about me that never can bear to be frightened at the will of others. My courage always rises at every attempt to intimidate me. ♥ Jane Austen

I have been driven many times to my knees by the overwhelming conviction that I had nowhere else to go. ♥ Abraham Lincoln

Believe there is great power silently working all things for good, behave yourself, and never mind the rest. ♡ Beatrix Potter

What would life be if we had no courage to attempt anything? ♥ Vincent Van Gogh

INSPIRATION

ITS ASTONISH
ING HOW SHORT
A TIME IT TAKES
FOR VERY WON
DERFUL THINGS
TO HAPPEN.
SEEK NOT OUT
SIDE YOURSELF.
HEAVEN IS
WITHIN

GO ♥ ON

REASONS TO LIVING

NOTHING
EVER STAYS
THE SAME • SOME •
THING GOOD COULD HAPPEN
Kitties • Snowstorms •
FUTURE BELLY LAUGHS •
Might KISS again • Driving in
car with windows
down & music up •   TEA
BOOKS • Art   CAKE
FLOWERS   Joy
• STARRY NIGHTS •   HUGS
                       trees
Hearing La Vie en Rose • BEAUTY •
NEW SHOES • FULL MOONS
• BEST FRIENDS & FAMILY •
FALLING LEAVES • BIRDSONG
LOBSTER   Wisteria
in BUTTER   in BLOOM
• Watercolor   Lunch with
spreading   Magazines
on wet paper •   NATURE
Alternative   redecorating
looks boring

DOGGIES AT THE DOOR

SOME   DAY
MIGHT SAIL ON AN OCEAN
LINER & GO TO EUROPE & FALL
IN LOVE • • DREAMING

Life always offers you a second chance. It's called TOMORROW. ♥ Stephen King

Go. Be.
Love.
The world
needs you. ♡

The sweetest flower that blows,
  I give you as we part.
For you it is a rose,
  For me it is my heart.

Frederick Peterson ♥

To be continued...